Pocket
SHÀNGHǍI
TOP SIGHTS · LOCAL LIFE · MADE EASY

Damian Harper

In This Book

QuickStart Guide

Your keys to understanding the city – we help you decide what to do and how to do it

Need to Know
Tips for a smooth trip

Neighbourhoods
What's where

Explore Shànghǎi

The best things to see and do, neighbourhood by neighbourhood

Top Sights
Make the most of your visit

Local Life
The insider's city

The Best of Shànghǎi

The city's highlights in handy lists to help you plan

Best Walks
See the city on foot

Shànghǎi's Best...
The best experiences

Survival Guide

Tips and tricks for a seamless, hassle-free city experience

Getting Around
Travel like a local

Essential Information
Including where to stay

Our selection of the city's best places to eat, drink and experience:

◎ **Sights**

✖ **Eating**

🍷 **Drinking**

✪ **Entertainment**

🔒 **Shopping**

These symbols give you the vital information for each listing:

📞 Telephone Numbers	👪 Family-Friendly
⌚ Opening Hours	🐾 Pet-Friendly
🅿 Parking	🚌 Bus
🚭 Nonsmoking	🚢 Ferry
@ Internet Access	Ⓜ Metro
🛜 Wi-Fi Access	🚊 Tram
🥗 Vegetarian Selection	🚆 Train
📖 English-Language Menu	

Find each listing quickly on maps for each neighbourhood:

Bar Hemingway

16 🍷 Map p233, B2

Legend has it that Hemi self, wielding a machine rate this timber-pan ered bar during showpiece is a en by Papa ar town. Dress s.com; Hôtel Rit ⌚6.30pm-2a

6 ◎ Plac Vo

Lonely Planet's Shànghǎi

Lonely Planet Pocket Guides are designed to get you straight to the heart of the city.

Inside you'll find all the must-see sights, plus tips to make your visit to each one really memorable. We've split the city into easy-to-navigate neighbourhoods and provided clear maps so you'll find your way around with ease. Our expert authors have searched out the best of the city: walks, food, nightlife and shopping, to name a few. Because you want to explore, our 'Local Life' pages will take you to some of the most exciting areas to experience the real Shànghǎi.

And of course you'll find all the practical tips you need for a smooth trip: itineraries for short visits, how to get around, and how much to tip the guy who serves you a drink at the end of a long day's exploration.

It's your guarantee of a really great experience.

Our Promise

You can trust our travel information because Lonely Planet authors visit the places we write about, each and every edition. We never accept freebies for positive coverage, so you can rely on us to tell it like it is.

QuickStart Guide **7**

Explore Shànghǎi **21**

Worth a Trip:

The Best of Shànghǎi 115

Shànghǎi's Best Walks

Shànghǎi's Best ...

Survival Guide 141

QuickStart Guide

Welcome to Shànghǎi

Positively electric, Shànghǎi is where China's aspirations come to life. A symbol of the country's burgeoning status, a byword for opportunity and sophistication, the city is all that and more. Whether you're after food, fashion or futuristic skylines, Shànghǎi's buzzing confidence and nonstop action make for a veritable roller-coaster ride: hang on to your hat, and have fun.

Tiánzǐfáng alleyway (p62)
TOM LAU / GETTY IMAGES ©

Shànghǎi Top Sights

The Bund (p24)

Mainland China's most iconic concession-era backdrop, the Bund encapsulates Shànghǎi with its postcard-perfect good looks. A dazzling curve of bombastic masonry, it leads the way as one of the city's most stylish addresses.

MANFRED GOTTSCHALK / GETTY IMAGES ©

Shànghǎi Museum (p28)

Shànghǎi's best museum by a long shot, this must-see is a marvellous tribute to the path of Chinese beauty throughout the millennia, from ancient bronzes and transcendent landscape paintings to gorgeous ceramic masterpieces.

ALAN COPSON / GETTY IMAGES ©

Yùyuán Gardens & Bazaar (p50)

For some, the Old Town's piecemeal charms are a must. This classical garden – a delightful array of traditional feng shui design features and history – is a fitting contrast to Shànghǎi's 'future now' mantra.

LONELY PLANET / GETTY IMAGES ©

Qībǎo (p112)

Should you tire of Shànghǎi's slick, international modernity, head for the quintessentially Chinese landscapes beyond the city centre. Qībǎo is the closest of the nearby canal towns, a mere half-hour away on the metro.

KP17010 / ALAMY STOCK PHOTO ©

XU ZHEN – PRODUCED BY MADEIN COMPANY, COURTESY OF ARTIST AND SHANGHART GALLERY IN M50

M50 (p94)

Located in a former cotton mill, industrially chic M50 is the city's main creative hub. Edgy galleries and occasional events make this an absorbing place to wander for anyone interested in art (and people watching).

Tiánzǐfáng (p62)

This engaging (and crowded) warren of *shíkùmén* (stone-gate house) architecture and hip boutiques is perfect for browsing while soaking up the flavours of the ever-elusive traditional Shànghǎi neighbourhood. Getting lost is half the fun.

Jade Buddha Temple (p92)

Despite first impressions, the city does have a strong current of religious tradition, best observed in this century-old Buddhist temple, which plays host to a continual stream of worshippers throughout the day.

Xīntiāndì (p64)

A visitor favourite, this prettified strip of traditional Shànghǎi housing is perhaps unique in its combination of fine dining, designer shopping, *shíkùmén* architecture and Chinese communist credentials (the CCP was born here).

Shànghǎi Local Life

Insider tips to help you find the real city

Shànghǎi is much more than the Bund and Xīntiāndì – to truly experience the city, you need to get under its skin, an experience best had by delving into small lanes, leafy side streets and old alleyways.

East Nanjing Road (p32)

▶ Historic shops
▶ People watching

Once China's most famous shopping street, East Nanjing Rd is perennially thick with eager shoppers, out-of-towners and neon signs illuminating the night. Take a deep breath, push your elbows out and plunge in.

Backstreets & Alleyways (p52)

▶ Temples
▶ Antique vendors

Explore the Old Town, following twisting alleyways and stopping to contemplate incense-wreathed temples along the way. There are some fantastic spots to pick up souvenirs, from faux antiques and local knick-knacks to tailor-made clothing.

Concession-Era Architecture (p78)

▶ Famous residences
▶ Cute boutiques

The French Concession's tree-lined lanes are a world away from Shànghǎi's busy central neighbourhoods. It's charming, European in feel and slower in tempo, so take the time to browse through the local boutiques and admire the stylistically diverse 19th-century villas as you go.

Jìng'ān Architecture (p96)

▶ Lǐlòng architecture
▶ Diverse shops

Away from the commercial buzz of the main drag (West Nanjing Rd), this area is charmingly detailed with pleasant *lǐlòng* (alleyways), its character supplied by a profusion of period architecture.

Hóngkǒu (p46)

▶ Local markets
▶ Street-side snacks

This gritty and somewhat run-down neighbourhood is off most tourist itineraries, but it's well worth a visit for its captivating street life and authentic vibe. Visit a local food market, a discount-clothing bazaar and the fabulous Concession-era architecture of the Shànghǎi Post Museum.

Taichi in Fùxīng Park (p68)

East Nanjing Road (p32)

Other great places to experience the city like a local:

Yang's Fry Dumplings (p41)

Jesse (p83)

Nánxiáng Steamed Bun Restaurant (p41)

Wujiang Road Food Street (p102)

Fùxīng Park (p68)

Din Tai Fung (p102)

Bǎinián Lóngpáo (p113)

Yongkang Road Bar Street (p73)

Yìfū Theatre (p44)

Shànghǎi Day Planner

Day One

One day in Shànghǎi? Rise with the sun for early-morning riverside views of the **Bund** (p24) as the city stirs from its slumber. Visit landmark buildings such as the **Fairmont Peace Hotel** (p44) and the **HSBC building** (p27) before strolling down **East Nanjing Road** (p32) to People's Square and the **Shànghǎi Museum** (p28) or the **Shànghǎi Urban Planning Exhibition Hall** (p36).

After a local lunch on **Yunnan Road Food Street** (p41), hop on the metro at People's Square to shuttle east to Pǔdōng. Explore the fun and interactive **Shànghǎi History Museum** (p108) or contemplate the Bund from the breezy **Riverside Promenade** (p109), and then take a high-speed lift to the super-high observation decks inside the **Shànghǎi Tower** (p107) or **Shànghǎi World Financial Center** (p107) to put the city in perspective.

As evening falls, return to the Bund for dinner. Try **Lost Heaven** (p38) for Yunnanese, **M on the Bund** (p40) for views or perhaps a simple meal at **Shànghǎi Grandmother** (p39). Afterwards, head to any of the nearby bars for cocktails or take an evening river **cruise** (p140).

Day Two

Two days? Pre-empt the crowds with an early start at the Old Town's **Yùyuán Gardens & Bazaar** (p50) before poking around for souvenirs along **Old Street** (p53). While you're wandering the alleyways, don't miss the **Chénxiānggé Nunnery** (p52) or the delightful neighbourhood around the **Confucius Temple** (p55).

Make your next stop **Xīntiāndì** (p64) for lunch – think five-star dumplings at **Din Tai Fung** (p70), dim sum at **Crystal Jade** (p71) or molecular creations at **T8** (p70). Don't linger over your meal for too long, however, as you'll need time to visit the **Shíkùmén Open House Museum** (p65) afterwards. From here, taxi it to **Tiánzǐfáng** (p62) for the afternoon, where you can browse start-up boutiques to your heart's content.

Stop by **Cafe des Stagiaires** (p72) for an aperitif before getting the evening's dinner sorted. The French Concession is absolutely bursting with choices, so do your homework first. Good picks are **Dī Shuǐ Dòng** (p70) and **Jian Guo 328** (p83). Afterwards, wind down with a **foot massage** (p131).

Short on time?
We've arranged Shànghǎi's must-sees into these day-by-day itineraries to make sure you see the very best of the city in the time you have available.

Day Three

It's another early start to the day – absorb the morning's clarity at **Jade Buddha Temple** (p92) before a visit to **M50** (p94), where you can plug into China's burgeoning modern-art scene. Still in a Buddhist frame of mind? Time for a meal at **Vegetarian Lifestyle** (p101).

From **Jìng'ān Temple** (p100) it's only one stop on the metro to the French Concession West, where you can check out some of the area's more obscure sights, such as the **Propaganda Poster Art Centre** (p81) or the old villas along **Wukang Road** (p78). If Shànghǎi's consumerism beckons, be sure to check out local fashion and vintage boutiques such as **NuoMi** (p88) and **Lolo Love Vintage** (p88).

Time for dinner – **Xībó** (p83) is a fine choice for Xīnjiāng cuisine, while Shanghainese classic **Jesse** (p83) is sure to offer a boisterous and lively atmosphere. You're in the right place to go out for a nightcap or hit the clubs; otherwise head back to Jìng'ān to spend an evening with the **acrobats** (p102).

Day Four

Most of the city's main sights have been checked off the list by now, so today offers the opportunity to visit some lesser-known areas. Begin the day strolling through the busy streets of **Hóngkǒu** (p46), which is also home to the **Ohel Moishe Synagogue** (p125) – now the Shànghǎi Jewish Refugees Museum.

If you need a break from the city, hop on the metro for a trip out to **Qībǎo** (p113), an erstwhile canal town and a popular destination for domestic tourists. Qībǎo has several low-key sights, but the main activity here is wandering among the old-style buildings – don't miss the teahouse with its traditional (albeit incomprehensible) storytelling performance. For an entirely different experience, head to the **AP Xīnyáng Fashion & Gifts Market** (p111) to fish for fresh- and saltwater pearls or pick up bargain T-shirts and shoes.

Time for one last blowout meal. For classy, old-fashioned ambience head to **Yè Shànghǎi** (p72) or **Fu 1039** (p84); alternatively, turn on the Sìchuān heat with a searing array of dishes at **Spicy Joint** (p83) or a delicious line of tapas at **Commune Social** (p100).

Need to Know

For more information, see Survival Guide (p141)

Currency
Rénmínbì (Yuán, ¥)

Language
Mandarin and Shanghainese

Visas
Seventy-two-hour visa-free transits available. Thirty-day single-entry visa standard for most nationalities. Longer visas are available, but can be a hassle to obtain.

Money
ATMs are widely available, but always carry some cash. High-end hotels, shops and restaurants generally accept credit cards.

Mobile Phones
Inexpensive pay-as-you-go SIM cards are available for unlocked GSM phones. Buying or renting a local phone is also an option.

Time
Chinese Standard Time (GMT/UTC plus eight hours)

Plugs & Adaptors
Three main pin styles: three-pronged angle pins (Australia), two flat pins (US, without the ground) and two round pins (Europe). Voltage 220V.

Tipping
Not practised in China. High-end restaurants and hotels include a 15% service charge in the bill, though hotel porters may expect a tip.

① Before You Go

Your Daily Budget

Budget less than ¥1400

▶ Double room at Chinese chain hotel ¥200–¥400

▶ Meal at mall food courts and tiny eateries ¥50

▶ One-day metro pass ¥18

Midrange ¥1400–¥2000

▶ Double room ¥1000–¥1500

▶ Good local dinner ¥150

▶ Cocktail at local bar ¥80

Top End more than ¥2000

▶ Luxury hotels ¥1500 and up

▶ Gastronomic dinner ¥300 and up

Useful Websites

Lonely Planet (www.lonelyplanet.com/china/shanghai) Destination information, bookings, traveller forum and more.

Smart Shanghai (www.smartshanghai.com) Listings website.

Time Out (www.timeoutshanghai.com) Listings website.

Ctrip (www.english.ctrip.com) Excellent online agency, good for hotel bookings.

Advance Planning

One month before Ensure visa and passport are in order. Check whether your trip will coincide with festivals or holidays and plan accordingly.

Two weeks before Consider possible itineraries and make restaurant reservations.

Two days before Learn how to count to 10 and say 'thank you' in Mandarin.

② Arriving in Shànghǎi

Shànghǎi has two main airports: Pǔdōng International Airport and Hóngqiáo Airport. Unless you are flying in from elsewhere in China, you'll arrive at Pǔdōng.

✈ From Pǔdōng International Airport

Destination	Best Transport
Bund	Metro line 2 or Maglev, then taxi
People's Square	Metro line 2 or Maglev, then taxi
Xīntiāndì (French Concession)	Maglev, then taxi or metro line 1, then line 2
Jing'ān Temple	Airport bus 2
Pǔdōng (Lujiazui)	Metro line 2 or Maglev, then taxi

✈ From Hóngqiáo Airport

Destination	Best Transport
Bund	Metro lines 2 or 10
People's Square	Metro line 2
Xīntiāndì (French Concession)	Metro line 10
Jing'ān Temple	Metro line 2
Pǔdōng (Lujiazui)	Metro line 2

🚗 Taxi

Taking a taxi from the Maglev terminus (Longyang Rd) is probably the fastest and easiest way into the city from Pǔdōng International Airport. It should cost you around ¥50 to ¥60 to downtown Shànghǎi.

③ Getting Around

Certain areas of Shànghǎi are more conducive to walking than others, but overall, walking through a Chinese city will wear you out faster than you expect. Although the metro is usually crowded, it's the best way to get around.

🚄 Maglev

The bullet-fast Shànghǎi Maglev will get you between Pǔdōng International Airport and Longyang Rd metro station (also in Pǔdōng), but not to downtown Shànghǎi.

Ⓜ Metro

Shànghǎi's ever-expanding metro system is indicated by a large red M. Lines 1, 2 and 10 are the most useful for travellers. Tickets cost between ¥3 and ¥15 depending on distance, and are sold from coin- and note-operated bilingual automated machines. Keep your ticket until you exit. One-/three-day metro passes (¥18/45) are sold at the airports and from some information desks. Most lines shut down by 10.30pm.

🚗 Taxi

Shànghǎi's taxis are reasonably cheap and easy to flag down (outside rush hour and rainstorms). Flag fall is ¥14 (for the first 3km) and ¥18 at night (11pm to 5am). To circumvent the language barrier, you *must* show the driver the Chinese address of your destination.

Look for the meter when you get in the car and ensure it is activated. Ask for a receipt (which has the driver and car number, useful if you leave something in the cab).

Shànghǎi Neighbourhoods

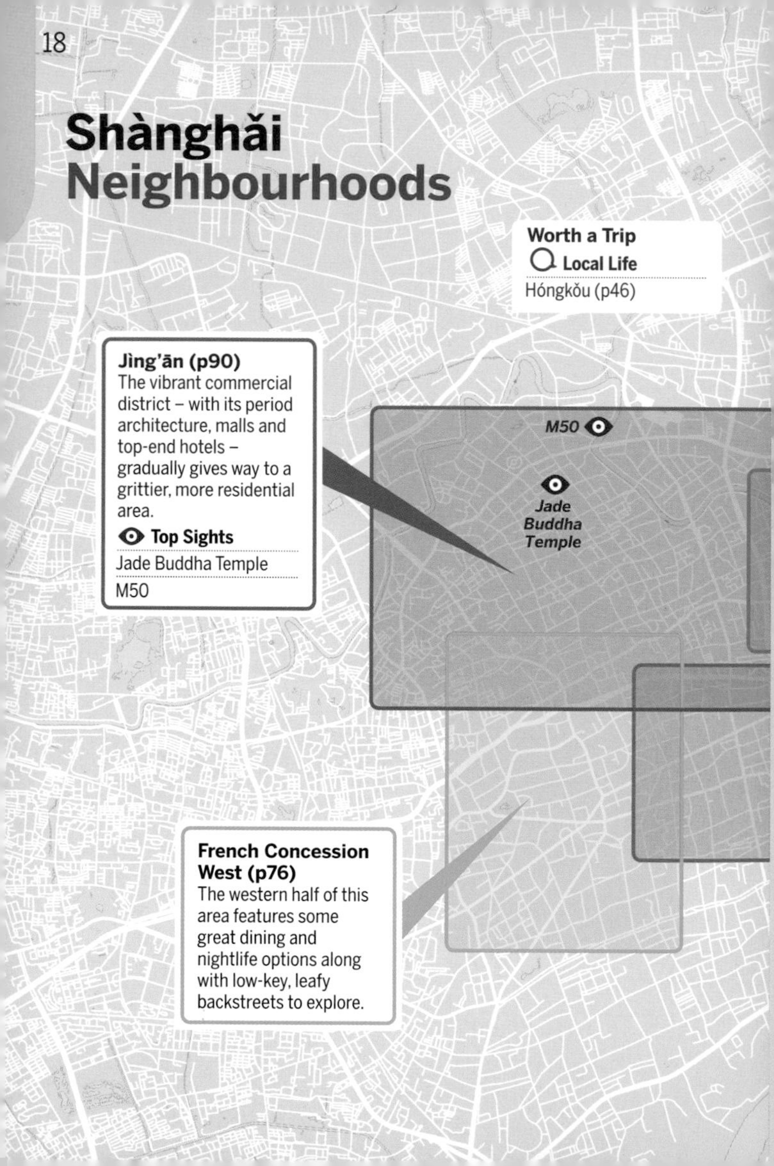

Worth a Trip
○ **Local Life**
Hóngkǒu (p46)

Jìng'ān (p90)
The vibrant commercial district – with its period architecture, malls and top-end hotels – gradually gives way to a grittier, more residential area.

◉ **Top Sights**
Jade Buddha Temple
M50

M50 ◉

◉ Jade Buddha Temple

French Concession West (p76)
The western half of this area features some great dining and nightlife options along with low-key, leafy backstreets to explore.

The Bund & People's Square (p22)
Magnificent colonial-era buildings and a clutch of top-notch museums make downtown Shànghǎi the first stop on everybody's list.

⊙ Top Sights
The Bund
Shànghǎi Museum

Pǔdōng (p104)
China's financial hub, Pǔdōng is a dazzling panorama of high-altitude hotels, banks, Maglev trains and giant television screens.

The Bund ⊙

Shànghǎi Museum ⊙

⊙ *Yùyuán Gardens & Bazaar*

⊙ *Xīntiāndì*

⊙ *Tiánzǐfáng*

Old Town (p48)
The original city core and the only part to predate the 1850s, the Old Town is a glimpse of 'traditional' China.

⊙ Top Sights
Yùyuán Gardens & Bazaar

French Concession East (p60)
The most stylish part of town, the former French Concession is where the bulk of Shànghǎi's disposable income is spent.

⊙ Top Sights
Tiánzǐfáng
Xīntiāndì

Worth a Trip
⊙ Top Sights
Qībǎo (p112)

Explore
Shànghǎi

Worth a Trip

Shànghǎi taxi
ARTUR DEBAT / GETTY IMAGES ©

Explore

The Bund & People's Square

Shànghǎi's standout spectacle, the Bund has emerged over the past decade into a designer retail and dining zone, and the city's most exclusive boutiques, restaurants and hotels see the strip as the only place to be. West of bustling East Nanjing Rd is People's Square, the de facto city centre, home to a clutch of museums, entertainment venues, malls and leafy parks.

The Sights in a Day

☼ Rise with the sun for early-morning riverside views of the **Bund** (p24) as the city stirs from its slumber. Visit landmark buildings such as the **Fairmont Peace Hotel** (p44) and the **HSBC building** (p27) or follow the **walking tour** (p116) through the North Bund area. From here, explore **East Nanjing Road** (p32) like a local, stopping off for lunch at **South Memory** (p41), **Yúxìn Chuāncài** (p38) or one of the area's standout **dumpling options** (p41).

☼ East Nanjing Rd leads to People's Square, famed for its museums. The star attraction is the **Shànghǎi Museum** (pictured left; 28) – you could easily spend the rest of the day here. Alternatively, the **Shànghǎi Urban Planning Exhibition Hall** (p36) makes for a fun browse.

☽ As evening falls, return to the Bund for dinner. Try **Lost Heaven** (p38) for Yunnanese, **Shànghǎi Grandmother** (p39) for home-style Chinese or **Mr & Mrs Bund** (p40) for French bistro food with a twist. Afterwards, head to any of the nearby bars for cocktails or take an evening river **cruise** (p140).

For a local's day in East Nanjing Road, see p32.

⊙ Top Sights

The Bund (p24)

Shànghǎi Museum (p28)

◗ Local Life

East Nanjing Road (p32)

♥ Best of Shànghǎi

Eating

Lost Heaven (p38)

Yang's Fry Dumplings (p41)

Nánxiáng Steamed Bun Restaurant (p41)

Yunnan Road Food Street (p41)

Mr & Mrs Bund (p40)

M on the Bund (p40)

Entertainment

Fairmont Peace Hotel Jazz Bar (p44)

Yìfū Theatre (p44)

Shànghǎi Grand Theatre (p44)

Getting There

Ⓜ **Metro** The Bund is a 10-minute walk east from the East Nanjing Rd stop (lines 2 and 10). People's Square station is served by lines 1, 2 and 8.

🚃 **Tourist Train** Runs along East Nanjing Rd's pedestrianised section (tickets ¥5) from Middle Henan Rd to Shànghǎi No 1 Department Store.

Top Sights
The Bund

Symbolic of colonial Shànghǎi, the Bund (外滩; Wàitān) was the city's Wall St, a place of feverish trading and fortunes made and lost. Coming to Shànghǎi and missing the Bund is like visiting Běijīng and bypassing the Forbidden City. Originally a towpath for dragging barges of rice, it's remained the first port of call for visitors since passengers began disembarking here more than a century ago, although today it's the trendy restaurants and views of Pǔdōng that beckon the crowds.

👁 Map p34, G2

East Zhongshan No 1 Rd; 中山东一路

Ⓜ East Nanjing Rd

The Shànghǎi skyline from the Bund

Don't Miss

The Promenade

The Bund offers a host of things to do, but most visitors head straight for the riverside promenade to pose for photos in front of Pǔdōng's continually morphing skyline across the river. The 1km walkway can be accessed anywhere in between Huángpǔ Park (the northern end) and the Meteorological Signal Tower (the southern end).

Huángpǔ Park

China's first public park (1868) achieved lasting notoriety for its apocryphal 'No Dogs or Chinese Allowed' sign. The park today is blighted by the anachronistic Monument to the People's Heroes, hiding the entrance to the **Bund History Museum** (外滩历史纪念馆; Wàitān Lìshǐ Jìniànguǎn; admission free; ⏱9am-4.30pm Mon-Fri), which shelters a small collection of old maps and photographs.

Jardine Matheson

Standing at No 27 on the Bund is the former headquarters of early opium trading company Jardine Matheson, which went on to become one of the most powerful trading houses in Hong Kong and Shànghǎi. Also known as EWO, it was the first foreign company to erect a building on the Bund in 1851. In 1941 the British Embassy occupied the top floor. Today it contains the House of Roosevelt, a huge wine cellar and bar.

Bank of China

A glorious meld of Chinese and Western architectural styling, this 1940s building (No 23) is a neat collision of art deco and Middle Kingdom motifs. Check out the funky deco Chinese lions out front. It was originally designed to be the tallest building in the city but wound up 1m shorter than its neighbour.

FEARGUS COONEY / GETTY IMAGES ©

☑ Top Tips

▶ The promenade is open around the clock, but it's at its best in the early morning, when locals are out practising taichi, or in the early evening, when both sides of the river are lit up and the majesty of the waterfront is at its grandest.

▶ You can arrange an hour-long tour (¥100) of the Bund's most famous monument, the Fairmont Peace Hotel, through the **Peace Gallery** (和平收藏馆; Hépíng Shōucángguǎn; Fairmont Peace Hotel, 20 East Nanjing Rd; 南京东路20号费尔蒙和平饭店; admission free; ⏱10.30am-7pm; Ⓜ East Nanjing Rd) in the lobby's mezzanine. Book a half-day in advance.

✖ Take a Break

There are plenty of fantastic drinking and dining options along the Bund, but if you're just looking for a seat, a decent coffee and a trendy vibe, head to Wagas (p42) on the corner of Jiujiang Rd and Middle Henan Rd.

Wàibáidù Bridge (Garden Bridge)

200 m
0.1 miles

Bund History Museum

Huángpǔ Park

E Beijing Rd
北京东路

Jardine Matheson

Bund Sightseeing Tunnel

Fairmont Peace Hotel

Bank of China

The Promenade

E Nanjing Rd
南京东路

Former Palace Hotel
Former Chartered Bank Building
North China Daily News Building

Jiujiang Rd
九江路

Huángpǔ River

Custom House

Hankou Rd
汉口路

Hongkong & Shanghai Bank Building

Fuzhou Rd
福州路

E Zhongshan No 1 Rd 中山东一路

Guangdong Rd
广东路

Three on the Bund

Meteorological Signal Tower

E Yan'an Rd
延安东路

Fairmont Peace Hotel

Victor Sassoon built Shànghǎi's most treasured art deco monument in the late '20s, when it was known as the Cathay Hotel. It was frequented by well-heeled celebrities (from George Bernard Shaw to Charlie Chaplin) – the riff-raff slept elsewhere. You don't need to be a guest, though, to admire the wonderful art deco lobby and rotunda or raise a glass to the old jazz band.

Former Palace Hotel

The former Palace Hotel was China's largest hotel when completed (1909), and hosted Sun Yatsen's 1911 victory celebration following his election as the first president of the Republic of China. Now a hotel run by Swatch, it's home to an artist's residency program.

Former Chartered Bank Building

Reopened a decade ago as the upscale entertainment complex Bund 18, the building boasts one of the Bund's premier late-night destinations: the top-floor Bar Rouge. The ground floor offers a sampler of the area's exclusive tastes, featuring a host of luxury brands.

North China Daily News Building

Known as the 'Old Lady of the Bund', the *News* ran from 1864 to 1951 as the main English-language newspaper in China. Look for the paper's motto above the central windows. The huge Atlas figures supporting the roof were designed in Italy and sculpted in Shànghǎi; each figure was carved from three blocks of granite.

Custom House

The Custom House (No 13), first established at this site in 1857 and rebuilt in 1927, has long been one of the most important buildings on the Bund. Capping the building is Big Ching, a bell modelled on London's Big Ben. During the Cultural Revolution, the bell was replaced with loudspeakers broadcasting revolutionary songs.

Hongkong & Shanghai Bank Building

Put a crick in your neck gawping at the ceiling mosaic portraying the 12 zodiac signs and the world's eight great banking centres. When it went up in 1923, the domed HSBC building was the second-largest bank in the world and commonly known as 'the finest building east of Suez'.

Three on the Bund

With its opening over a decade ago, Three on the Bund became the strip's first lifestyle destination and the model that many other Bund edifices have since followed. Upscale restaurants and bars occupy the upper three floors, while the lower levels are anchored by Armani, the Evian Spa and the conceptually minded Shànghǎi Gallery of Art (p38).

Meteorological Signal Tower

This **signal tower** (外滩信号台; Wàitān Xìnhào Tái; 1 East Zhongshan No 2 Rd; 中山东二路1号; admission free; ⊙10am-5pm; M East Nanjing Rd) was built in 1907 to replace the wooden original, as well as to serve as a meteorological relay station for the tireless Shànghǎi Jesuits. The tower was shut at the time of writing and until recently contained a cafe on its upper floors.

Restaurants

There's no shortage of upscale Western restaurants here, many of which sport fabulous views. Top choices are Mr & Mrs Bund (p40) at Bund 18 and M on the Bund (p40). Lost Heaven (p38) has the finest Chinese cuisine in the area, though unfortunately no panoramas.

Nightlife

If cocktails are your thing, you're spoilt for choice: decadent watering holes include the Long Bar (p42), Sir Elly's Terrace (p42), New Heights (p42) and Bar Rouge (p42). For flavours of historical Shànghǎi, the Fairmont Peace Hotel (p44) has its old-fashioned Jazz Bar, serenading punters nightly from 7pm.

Top Sights
Shànghǎi Museum

An invigorating shot of adrenaline into the leaden legs of Chinese museum-goers, the Shànghǎi Museum houses a stupefying collection of the cream of the millennia, all under one roof. Exhibits cover the high watermarks of Chinese civilisation, from the meditative beauty of landscape paintings to the exquisite perfection of a celadon vase. Thorough English captions, a light-filled atrium and well-spaced exhibits are all arcs on an enticing learning curve.

👁 Map p34, C5

www.shanghaimuseum.net

上海博物馆; Shànghǎi Bówùguǎn

201 Renmin Ave; 人民大道201号

admission free

🕑9am-5pm

Ⓜ People's Sq

Don't Miss

Ancient Chinese Bronzes Gallery

On the ground floor is the Shànghǎi Museum's star attraction, an unrivalled collection of ancient bronzes, some of which date as far back as the 21st century BC. The remarkable diversity of shapes is striking, revealing the significance of bronze in early society. Objects include sacrificial vessels, wine jars, weapons, two-toned bells and more.

Ancient Chinese Sculpture Gallery

This ground-floor gallery's exhibits range from the funeral sculptures of the Qin and Han dynasties to the predominantly Buddhist sculptures of the following centuries, which were heavily influenced by the Indian and Central Asian styles that came to China via the Silk Road. A must for those interested in Buddhist artwork.

Ancient Chinese Ceramics Gallery

On the 2nd floor, this is one of the largest and most fascinating galleries in the museum. Don't worry if you don't know your 'ewer with overhead handles in *dòucǎi* (斗彩)' from your 'brush-holder with *fěncǎi* (粉彩) design'; it's all part of a magnificent introduction to this rich tradition. Highlights include the Tang tricolour pottery and Song-dynasty tableware.

Chinese Painting Gallery

This gallery leads visitors through various styles of traditional Chinese painting, from hanging and horizontal scrolls to album leaflets that depict nature in miniature. Look for works by masters such as Ni Zan (1301–74), Wang Meng (1308–85) and Qiu Ying (1494–1552), and compare the impressive array of brush techniques used over the centuries.

☑ **Top Tips**

▶ It's best to arrive in the morning, as only 8000 people are allowed in daily and the lines can quickly get long.

▶ Before you enter the museum, admire the exterior of the building. Designed to recall an ancient bronze *dǐng* (鼎; three-legged ritual vessel), the building also echoes the shape of a famous bronze mirror from the Han dynasty, exhibited within the museum.

▶ The audio guide is well worth the ¥40 fee (¥400 deposit, or your passport). It highlights particularly interesting items within an exhibit and offers good gallery overviews.

✗ **Take a Break**

There's a simple restaurant on the ground floor and a cafe on the 2nd floor if you need a break, but the best place for a real meal is outside the museum, at the nearby Yunnan Road Food Street.

SERGIO AZENHA / ALAMY STOCK PHOTO ©

Jade pieces in the Ancient Chinese Jade Gallery

Seals (chops) are notable both for the intricacy of their design and the special script used on the underside, which is known to only a handful of artisans and calligraphers. Look for the two orange soapstone seals that feature incredibly detailed landscapes in miniature.

Minority Nationalities Art Gallery
Save some energy for the Minority Nationalities Art Gallery, which introduces visitors to the diversity of China's non-Han ethnic groups, totalling (officially) some 40 million people. Displays focus mainly on dress, from the salmon-skin suit from Hēilóngjiāng and the furs of the Siberian Oroqen to the embroidery and batik of Guìzhōu's Miao and Dong.

Ming & Qing Furniture Gallery
This 4th-floor gallery features elegant rose- and sandalwood furniture from the Ming dynasty, and heavier, more baroque examples from the succeeding Qing dynasty. Several mock offices and reception rooms offer a glimpse into wealthy Chinese home life.

Ancient Chinese Jade Gallery
The most important precious stone in China, jade use dates back some 5000 years. This gallery introduces pieces such as ritual weapons, jewellery, early mystical totems and symbols – such as the *bì* (璧) or 'jade discs', used to worship heaven. Bamboo drills, abrasive sand and garnets crushed in water were used to shape the pieces.

Chinese Calligraphy Gallery
Chinese characters, which express both meaning as a word and visual beauty as an image, are one of the language's most fascinating aspects. While the full scope of this gallery may be unfathomable for those who don't read Chinese, anyone can enjoy the purely aesthetic balance of the brush artistry, much of which dates back hundreds of years.

Chinese Seal Gallery
Although obscure, this gallery provides a fascinating glimpse into the niche art form of miniature carving.

Shànghǎi Museum

4th Floor

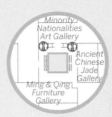

Minority
Nationalities
Art Gallery

Ancient
Chinese
Jade
Gallery

Ming & Qing
Furniture
Gallery

3rd Floor

Chinese Painting
Gallery

Chinese
Calligraphy
Gallery

Chinese
Seal
Gallery

2nd Floor

Cafe

Ancient
Chinese
Ceramics
Gallery

People's Square
Exit

Ground Floor

Ancient
Chinese
Bronzes
Gallery

Ancient
Chinese
Sculpture
Gallery

Audio
Guides

Gift
Shop

Audio
Guides

Restaurant

Main Entrance

Local Life
East Nanjing Road

Running between the Bund and People's Square is this shopping strip, which originally rose to prominence in the 1920s as the site of China's first department stores. A glowing forest of neon at night, it's no longer the cream of Shànghǎi shopping, but its pedestrian section is still one of the most famous and crowded streets in China.

❶ Noodles & Hotpot

Rising above the East Nanjing Rd metro station is the seven-storey **Hóngyī Plaza** (宏伊国际广场; Hóngyī Guójì Guǎngchǎng; 299 East Nanjing Rd, 南京东路299号; meals from ¥30; 🔌; Ⓜ East Nanjing Rd), which anchors the eastern end of the pedestrian strip. While the shopping is nothing to crow about, there are some fabulous eating options, which are always bustling at mealtimes. Head to the basement for snacks.

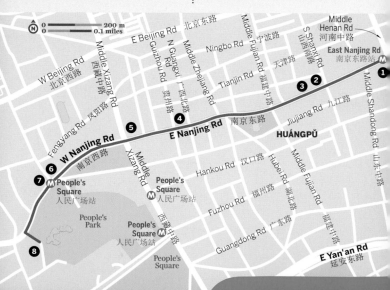

② Traditional Art

Duǒyúnxuān Art Shop (朵云轩; Duǒyún Xuān; 📞021 6360 6475; 422 East Nanjing Rd; 南京东路422号; ⏰9.30am-9.30pm; Ⓜ East Nanjing Rd) is a traditional-looking building (look for the two enormous calligraphy brushes outside) with an excellent selection of art and calligraphy supplies. The 2nd floor is wonderful for art books, while the 3rd floor houses antiques and some excellent calligraphy and brush-painting galleries.

③ Traditional Chinese Medicine

Opened in 1882, **Cai Tong De** (450 East Nanjing Rd; 南京东路450号) is one of the oldest and most famous traditional pharmacies in Shànghǎi. There's a clinic and herbal pharmacy on the top floor (no English), while the ground floor carries speciality items such as ginseng, caterpillar fungus and acupuncture supplies.

④ No 1 Food Store

This **store** (第一食品商店; Dìyī Shípǐn Shāngdiàn; 720 East Nanjing Rd; 南京东路720号; Ⓜ People's Sq) is bedlam, but this is how the Shanghainese shop and it's lots of fun. Trawl the ground floor for dried mushrooms, sea cucumbers, moon cakes and dried fruit. Built in 1926 and renovated in 2012, this used to be Sun Sun, one of Shànghǎi's big department stores.

⑤ Shànghǎi No 1 Department Store

Opened in 1936, this **department store** (上海市第一百货商店; Shànghǎi Shì Dìyī Bǎihuò Shāngdiàn; 800 East Nanjing Rd; 南京东路800号; ⏰9.30am-10pm; Ⓜ People's Sq) was formerly known as the Sun Company and was one of East Nanjing Rd's big department stores (with Wing On, Sun Sun and Sincere) and the first equipped with an escalator. It averages 150,000 shoppers a day.

⑥ Park Hotel

Designed by Hungarian architect Ladislaus Hudec and erected as a bank in 1934, the Park Hotel was Shànghǎi's tallest building until the 1980s, when architects first started squinting hopefully in the direction of Pǔdōng. Back in the day, it was said your hat would fall off if you looked at the roof.

⑦ Grand Theatre

West of the Park Hotel, the Grand Theatre is another East Nanjing Rd art deco veteran and another design by prolific architect Ladislaus Hudec. It was Shànghǎi's standout theatre in the 1930s and seated 1913 people.

⑧ Former Shànghǎi Raceclub Building

Until recently, the former Shànghǎi Raceclub Building (1934) housed the Shànghǎi Art Museum, but during its concession-era heyday, the elegant edifice, with its 10-storey tower, lorded it over the horse-racing track, whose grounds became People's Park.

E F G H

N Suzhou Rd 苏州北路
S Suzhou Rd 南苏州路 河南中路

Huqiu Rd
Yuanmingyuan Rd
Middle Sichuan Rd
Middle Jiangxi Rd

1
Rockbund
Art Museum 北京东路
18 ⊕

7 **16** ⊕

Bund
Sightseeing Tunnel

E Beijing Rd
四川中路

Dianchi Rd 滇池路

20 ⭐

E Zhongshan No 1 Rd 中山东一路

Huángpǔ River

Vingbo Rd S Shanxi Rd 天津路
Tianjin Rd

East Nanjing Rd
南京东路站 Ⓜ

E Nanjing Rd 南京东路

9 ⊗

ℹ️

◉ **The Bund**

12 Ⓜ
13 ⊗
江西中路
Jiujiang Rd 九江路

Jiujiang Rd
6
Hankou Rd
河南中路

Middle Henan Rd Middle Shandong Rd

Hankou Rd

8 ⊗

23 🔒 **22** 🔒

19 ⊕
14 ⊗

Fuzhou Rd 福州路

Middle Sichuan Rd

10 ⊕
Shànghǎi
Gallery of Art ◉
4 ⊕ **15**

East Yan'an Rd Tunnel

HUÁNGPǓ

Hubei Rd Middle Fujian Rd 福建中路

山东中路 河南中路

Guangdong Rd 广东路

E Yan'an Rd 延安东路

5 ⊗

E Zhongshan No 2 Rd
中山东二路

湖北路
东路 S Fujian Rd 宁海东路 金陵东路
E Ninghai Rd E Jinling Rd 福建南路

Renmin Rd
人民路

Yongshou Rd Yunnan Rd
11 ⊗

Yuyuan
Ⓜ **Garden**
豫园站

For reviews see
◉	Top Sights	p24
◉	Sights	p36
⊗	Eating	p38
⊕	Drinking	p42
⭐	Entertainment	p44
🔒	Shopping	p45

Ⓝ 0 —— 500 m
0 —— 0.25 miles

OLIVIER CHOUCHANA / GETTY IMAGES ©

Q Confucius No. 2 by Zhang Huan at the Rockbund Art Museum

Sights

Rockbund Art Museum · MUSEUM

1 ◉ Map p34, G1

Housed in the former Royal Asiatic Society building (1933) – the site of Shànghǎi's first museum – this private space behind the Bund focuses on contemporary Chinese art, with rotating exhibits year-round and no permanent collection. Check out the unique art deco eight-sided *bāguà* (trigram) windows at the front, a fetching synthesis of Western modernist styling and traditional Chinese design. (上海外滩美术馆; Shànghǎi Wàitān Měishùguǎn; www.rockbundartmuseum.org; 20 Huqiu Rd; 虎丘路20号; adult ¥15; ⊙10am-6pm Tue-Sun; Ⓜ East Nanjing Rd)

Shànghǎi Urban Planning Exhibition Hall · MUSEUM

2 ◉ Map p34, C4

Some cities romanticise their past; others promise good times in the present. Only in China are you expected to visit places that haven't even been built yet. The highlight here is the 3rd floor, where you'll find an incredible model layout of the megalopolis-to-be, plus a dizzying Virtual World 3D wraparound tour. Balancing out the forward-looking exhibits are photos and maps of historic Shànghǎi. (上海城市规划展示馆; Shànghǎi Chéngshì Guīhuà Zhǎnshìguǎn; 100 Renmin Ave, entrance on Middle Xizang Rd; 人民大道100号; adult ¥30; ⊙9am-5pm Tue-Sun, last entry 4pm; Ⓜ People's Sq)

Understand

The Opium Trade & the Foreign Concessions

Although Shànghǎi had served as a port city since the 14th century, the seeds of its future as an international trading hub weren't sown until the late 18th century, when British traders based in Canton (Guǎngzhōu) began importing opium to trade for silver. The highly addictive drug rapidly permeated all levels of Chinese society, with *hongs* (trading houses) such as Jardine Matheson built upon its trade.

Smouldering friction between Great Britain and China over the drug finally erupted in the conflict fought in its name: the First Opium War. The Treaty of Nanking (1842) that concluded the hostilities opened five ports, including Shànghǎi and Canton, to the West.

The Concessions

Shànghǎi's port was the most prosperous due to its superb location, capital edge and marginal interference from the Chinese government. Great Britain's arrival in Shànghǎi, dating from 1843, was soon followed by that of other nations. Trade quickly flourished as the area outside the Old Town was divided into British, French and American Concessions. The original British Concession included the Bund and the area extending due west to today's People's Square; the American Concession was established shortly thereafter to the north in Hóngkǒu. These two concessions later joined to form one large area known as the International Settlement. The French settlement began to the south with a sliver of land wedged between the British Concession and the Chinese town (now the Old Town) but later developed inland, eventually giving rise to the area still known by foreigners as the French Concession.

Growth

Trade of silk, tea, textiles, porcelain and opium was matched by rapidly developing banking, insurance and real-estate sectors. China and the West traded with each other via Chinese middlemen called *compradors* (from the Portuguese). Lured by the sense of opportunity, immigrants from other parts of China began to arrive. The city found itself propelled into a new era of gaslight, electricity and cars, and became the foremost agent of modernisation and change in post-imperial China.

Shànghǎi Museum of Contemporary Art (MOCA Shànghǎi)

MUSEUM

3 Map p34, C4

This nonprofit museum collection has an all-glass home to maximise natural sunlight when it cuts through the clouds, a tip-top location in People's Park and a fresh, invigorating approach to exhibiting contemporary artwork. Exhibits are temporary only; check the website to see what's on. On the top floor there's a funky restaurant and bar with a terrace. (上海当代艺术馆; Shànghǎi Dāngdài Yìshùguǎn; www.mocashanghai.org; People's Park; 人民公园; adult/student ¥50/25; ⊙10am-6pm Mon-Thu, 9am-7pm Fri-Sun; Ⓜ People's Sq)

Shànghǎi Gallery of Art

GALLERY

4 Map p34, H3

Take the lift up to the 3rd floor of Three on the Bund to this neat and minimalist art gallery for glimpses of current directions in highbrow and conceptual Chinese art. It's all bare concrete pillars, ventilation ducts and acres of wall space; there are a couple of divans where you can sit to admire the works on view. (外滩三号沪申画廊; Wàitān Sānhào Hùshēn Huàláng; www.shanghaigalleryofart.com; 3rd fl, Three on the Bund, 3 East Zhongshan No 1 Rd; 中山东一路三号三楼; admission free; ⊙11am-7pm; Ⓜ East Nanjing Rd)

Eating

Lost Heaven

YUNNAN $$

5 Map p34, H4

Lost Heaven mightn't have the views that keep its rivals in business, but why go to the same old Western restaurants when you can get sophisticated Bai, Dai and Miao folk cuisine from China's mighty southwest? Specialities are flowers (banana and pomegranate), wild mushrooms, chillies, Burmese curries, Bai chicken and superb *pǔ'ěr* (pu-erh) teas, served up in gorgeous Yúnnán-meets-Shànghǎi surrounds. (花马天堂; Huāmǎ Tiāntáng; ☏ 021 6330 0967; www.lostheaven.com.cn; 17 East Yan'an Rd; 延安东路17号; dishes ¥50-210; ⊙noon-2pm & 5.30-10.30pm; ⊙; Ⓜ East Nanjing Rd)

Yúxìn Chuāncài

SICHUANESE $

6 Map p34, E3

In the top league of Shànghǎi's best Sìchuān restaurants, Yúxìn is a dab hand at the arts of blistering chillies and numbing peppercorns. All-stars include the 'mouth-watering chicken' starter (口水鸡; *kǒushuǐ jī*), the simply smoking spicy chicken (辣子鸡; *làzǐ jī*), the crispy camphor tea duck (half/whole ¥38/68) and catfish in chilli oil. (渝信川菜; ☏ 021 6361 1777; 5th fl, Huasheng Tower, 399 Jiujiang Rd; 九江路399号华盛大厦5楼; dishes ¥20-98; ⊙11am-2.30pm & 5-9.30pm; ⊙⊙; Ⓜ East Nanjing Rd)

Shànghǎi Museum Art Store (p45)

Lobby, Peninsula Hotel
BRITISH $$$

7 Map p34, G1

Afternoon heritage tea for visitors in smart-casual attire in the sumptuous Peninsula lobby is a delight, with gorgeously presented scones, macaroons, clotted cream, jam, cookies, tea and live piano tinklings. For ¥440, a glass of champers is thrown in. Come evening, a live jazz band takes over. You can dine here all day à la carte from 6am to midnight. (上海半岛酒店; Shànghǎi Bàndǎo Jiǔdiàn; http://shanghai. peninsula.com; 32 E Zhongshan No 1 Rd; 中山东一路32号; 1/2 persons ¥290/540; ⊗2-6pm; 🛜📶; MEast Nanjing Rd)

Shànghǎi Grandmother
CHINESE $

8 Map p34, G3

This packed eatery is within easy striking distance of the Bund and cooks up all manner of homestyle dishes. You can't go wrong with the classics here: braised eggplant in soya sauce, Grandmother's braised pork, crispy duck, three-cup chicken and *mápó dòufu* (麻婆豆腐; tofu and pork crumbs in a spicy sauce) rarely disappoint. (上海姥姥; Shànghǎi Lǎolao; 📞021 6321 6613; 70 Fuzhou Rd; 福州路70号; dishes ¥25-55; ⊗10.30am-9.30pm; 📶; MEast Nanjing Rd)

Mr & Mrs Bund
FRENCH $$$

9 🍴 Map p34, G2

French chef Paul Pairet's casual eatery aims for a space considerably more playful than your average fine-dining Bund restaurant. The mix-and-match menu has a heavy French-bistro slant, but reimagined and served up with Pairet's ingenious presentation. But it's not just the food you're here for, it's the postmidnight meals (discounted), the Bingo nights and the wonderfully wonky atmosphere. Reserve. (📞021 6323 9898; www.mmbund.com; 6th fl, Bund 18, 18 East Zhongshan No 1 Rd; 中山东一路18号6楼; mains ¥150-800, 2-/3-course set lunch ¥200/250; ⏰lunch 11.30am-2pm Mon-Fri, dinner 6-11pm Fri & Sat, 6-10.30pm Sun-Thu, night 10.30pm-2am Tue-Thu, 11pm-2am Fri & Sat; 🚇; Ⓜ East Nanjing Rd)

M on the Bund
EUROPEAN $$$

10 🍴 Map p34, H3

M exudes a timelessness and a level of sophistication that eclipse the razzle-dazzle of many other upscale Shànghǎi restaurants. The menu ain't radical, but that's the question it seems to ask you – is breaking new culinary ground really so crucial? Crispy suckling pig and a chicken tajine with saffron are, after all, simply delicious just the way they are. (米氏西餐厅; Mǐshì Xīcāntīng; 📞021 6350 9988; www.m-restaurantgroup.com/mbund/home.html; 7th fl, 20 Guangdong Rd; 广东路20号7楼; mains ¥128-288, 2-course set lunch ¥188, light lunch menu ¥118; 🚇; Ⓜ East Nanjing Rd)

Shaanxi dumplings

Yunnan Road Food Street

CHINESE

11 🍴 Map p34, E5

Yunnan Rd has great speciality restaurants and is the spot for an authentic meal after museum-hopping at People's Square. Look out for Shaanxi dumplings and noodles at No 15 and five-fragrance dim sum at **Wǔ Fāng Zhāi** (五芳斋; 28 Yunnan Rd; 云南路28号; ⏱7am-10pm). You can also get salted duck (盐水鸭; *yán shuǐ yā*) and steamed dumplings at **Xiǎo Jīn Líng** (小金陵; 55 Yunnan Rd; 云南路55号; dumplings from ¥7; ⏱8am-9pm), as well as Mongolian hotpot and Yunnanese. (云南路美食街; Yúnnán Lù Měishí Jiē; Ⓜ Dashijie)

Mercato

ITALIAN $$

Located in the same building as the Shànghǎi Gallery of Art (see 4 ◎ Map p34, H3), Chef Jean-Georges Vongerichten's celebrated Bund-side restaurant combines first-rate (and affordable) Italian cuisine with a stylishly relaxed Neri & Hu–designed setting of modern rusticity. Add an exacting level of service for an experience to savour. The rigatoni and meatballs is a faultless pleasure, while pizzas (starting at ¥68) provide a masterclass in taste and texture. Reserve, especially for a window table. (☎ 021 6321 9922; 6th fl, Three on the Bund, 3 East Zhongshan No 1 Rd; 中山东一路3号6楼; mains ¥68-228; ⏱5.30-11pm Sun-Wed, to 1am Thu-Sat; 🛜 📶; Ⓜ East Nanjing Rd)

South Memory

HUNANESE $

12 🍴 Map p34, F2

This popular place a chopstick's throw from the waterfront has a range of spicy dry pots (served in personal miniwoks), including favourites bamboo shoots and smoked pork, and chicken and chestnuts. Also on the menu are other *xiāngcài* (Hunanese) classics (such as steamed pork served in a bamboo tube). It's jammed at lunchtime and only early birds get window seats. (望湘园; Wàng Xiāng Yuán; ☎ 021 6360 2797; 6th fl, Hóngyī Plaza, 299 East Nanjing Rd; 南京东路299号宏伊国际广场6楼; dishes ¥29-88; 📶; Ⓜ East Nanjing Rd)

Wagas

CAFE $

13 Map p34, F2

Just south off East Nanjing Rd, this branch of the city's favourite cafe is perfect for on-the-spot caffeination, sandwiches, wraps, pasta and Asian sets. (沃歌斯; Wògēsī; 1st fl, Hóngyì Plaza, 288 Jiujiang Rd, 九江路288号宏伊国际广场1楼; mains ¥48-58; ⏰6.30am-10pm Mon-Fri, 8.30am-10pm Sat & Sun; 🚇🛜📶; Ⓜ East Nanjing Rd)

Tock's

CANADIAN $

14 Map p34, F3

Unsurprisingly, this is the sole place in town serving Montreal-style smoked meat, but Shànghǎi could sorely do with more of the same. The meat – spiced and cured Australian beef, slow-smoked locally – is gorgeously tender and each sandwich comes with homemade fries, coleslaw and pickle. Canadian Moosehead lager and organic coffee is at hand for lubrication. (221 Middle Henan Rd; 河南中路221号; mains from ¥45; ⏰11am-10.30pm; 📶; Ⓜ East Nanjing Rd)

Drinking

Long Bar

BAR

15 Map p34, H3

For a taste of colonial-era Shànghǎi's elitist trappings, you'll do no better than the Long Bar. This was once the members-only Shànghǎi Club, whose most spectacular accoutrement was a 34m-long wooden bar. Foreign businessmen would sit here according to rank, comparing fortunes, with the taipans (foreign heads of business) closest to the view of the Bund. (廊吧; Láng Bā; ☏021 6322 9988; 2 East Zhongshan No 1 Rd; 中山东一路2号; ⏰4pm-1am Mon-Sat, 2pm-1am Sun; 🛜; Ⓜ East Nanjing Rd)

New Heights

BAR

The most amenable of the big Bund bars, this rooftop terrace in the same building as the Shànghǎi Gallery of Art (see **4** ◎ Map p34, H3), has the choicest angle on Pǔdōng's hypnotising neon performance. There's always a crowd, whether for coffee, cocktails or meals (set meals from ¥188). (新视角; Xīn Shìjiǎo; ☏021 6321 0909; 7th fl, Three on the Bund, 3 East Zhongshan No 1 Rd; 中山东一路3号7楼; ⏰11.30am-1.30am; Ⓜ East Nanjing Rd)

Bar Rouge

BAR

Located one floor up from Mr & Mrs Bund (see **9** Map p34, G2), Bar Rouge attracts a cashed-up party crowd that comes for the fantastic views from the terrace and the all-night DJ parties. The lipstick-red decor is slick and the crowd is slicker, so ordinary mortals can sometimes struggle to be served on busy nights. (☏021 6339 1199; 7th fl, Bund 18, 18 East Zhongshan No 1 Rd; 中山东一路18号7楼; cover charge after 10pm Fri & Sat ¥100; ⏰6pm-late; Ⓜ East Nanjing Rd)

Sir Elly's Terrace

BAR

16 Map p34, G1

Offering some of Shànghǎi's best cocktails, shaken up with that

Běijīng Opera, a traditional form of Chinese theatre (p44)

winning ingredient: 270-degree views to Pǔdōng, over Suzhou Creek and down the Bund. Of course it's not cheap, but the views are priceless. (艾利爵士露台; Àilì Juéshì Lùtái; 14th fl, The Peninsula Shanghai, 32 East No 1 Zhongshan Rd; 中山东一路32号半岛酒店14楼; ⏰5pm-midnight Sun-Thu, to 1am Fri & Sat; 🛜📶; ⓂEast Nanjing Rd)

Barbarossa
BAR
17 Map p34, B4

Set back in People's Park alongside a pond, Barbarossa is pure escapism. Forget Shànghǎi, this is Morocco channelled via Hollywood. The action grows more intense as you ascend

to the roof terrace, via the cushion-strewn 2nd floor, where hordes puff on hookahs. At night, use the park entrance just east of the former Shànghǎi Raceclub building (上海跑马总会; Shànghǎi Pǎomǎ Zǒnghuì). (芭芭露莎会所; Bābālùshā Huìsuǒ; www. barbarossa.com.cn; People's Park, 231 West Nanjing Rd; 南京西路231号人民公园内; ⏰11am-2am; 🛜; ⓂPeople's Sq)

Muse
CLUB
18 Map p34, G1

One of the hottest clubs in the city for more than six years now – and that's no small feat – Muse has moved downtown to this swanky Bund-side

Local Life
Chinese Opera

Just east of People's Square, the **Yìfū Theatre** (Map p34, D4; 逸夫舞台; Yifū Wǔtái; ☑021 6322 5294; www.tianchan.com; 701 Fuzhou Rd; 人民广场福州路701号; tickets ¥30-280; Ⓜ People's Square) has Kunqu and Yue (Shaoxing) opera on the program, with a Běijīng opera highlights show performed several times a week at 1.30pm and 7.15pm. Pick up a brochure at the ticket office.

location. Don't go looking for a lot of dance space; just squeeze into the crowd or jump up on a private table (minimum ¥4000 per night). (☑021 5213 5228; 5th fl, Yi Feng Galleria, 99 East Beijing Rd; 北京东路99号5楼; Ⓜ East Nanjing Rd)

M1NT
CLUB

19 Map p34, F3

Exclusive penthouse-style club with knockout views and snazzy fusion food but not a lot of dance space. Dress to impress or you'll get thrown into the shark tank. (☑021 6391 2811; 24th fl, 318 Fuzhou Rd; 福州路318号24楼; ☉lounge 6pm-late daily, club 9pm-late Wed-Sat; Ⓜ East Nanjing Rd)

Entertainment

Fairmont Peace Hotel Jazz Bar
JAZZ

20 Map p34, G2

Shànghǎi's most famous hotel features Shànghǎi's most famous jazz band, a septuagenarian sextet that's been churning out nostalgic covers such as 'Moon River' and 'Summertime' since the dawn of time. There's no admission fee, but you'll need to sink a drink from the bar (draught beer starts at ¥70, a White Lady is ¥98). (爵士吧; Juéshì Bā; ☑021 6138 6883; 20 East Nanjing Rd; 南京东路20号费尔蒙和平饭店; ☉5.30pm-2am, live music from 7pm; Ⓜ East Nanjing Rd)

Shànghǎi Grand Theatre
CLASSICAL MUSIC

21 ⭐ Map p34, B4

Shànghǎi's state-of-the-art concert venue hosts everything from Broadway musicals to symphonies, ballets, operas and performances by internationally acclaimed classical soloists. There are also traditional Chinese music performances here. Pick up a schedule at the ticket office. (上海大剧院; Shànghǎi Dàjùyuàn; ☑021 6386 8686; www.shgtheatre.com; 300 Renmin Ave; 人民广场人民大道300号; Ⓜ People's Sq)

Shopping

Annabel Lee
ACCESSORIES

22 🔒 Map p34, G3

This elegant shop sells a range of soft-coloured accessories in silk, linen and cashmere, many of which feature delicate and stylish embroidery. Peruse the collection of shawls, scarves, table runners, purses, evening bags and nighties. (安梨家居; Ānlí Jiājū; No 1, Lane 8, East Zhongshan No 1 Rd; 中山东一路8弄1号; ⏰10am-10pm; M East Nanjing Rd)

Sūzhōu Cobblers
ACCESSORIES

23 🔒 Map p34, G3

Right off the Bund, this cute boutique sells exquisite hand-embroidered silk slippers, bags, hats and clothing. Patterns and colours are based on the fashions of the 1930s, and as far as the owner, Huang Mengqi, is concerned, the products are one of a kind. Slippers start at ¥480 and the shop can make to order. (上海起想艺术品; Shànghǎi Qǐxiǎng Yìshùpǐn; unit 101, 17 Fuzhou Rd; 福州路17号101室; ⏰10am-6.30pm; M East Nanjing Rd)

Shànghǎi Museum Art Store
GIFTS

24 🔒 Map p34, C5

Attached to the Shànghǎi Museum and entered from East Yan'an Rd, this store offers a refreshing change from the usual tourist tat. Apart from the excellent range of books on Chinese art and architecture, there's a good selection of quality cards, prints and slides. The annexe shop sells fine imitations of some of the museum's ceramic pieces, as well as accessories. (上海博物馆艺术品商店; Shànghǎi Bówùguǎn Yìshùpǐn Shāngdiàn; 201 Renmin Ave; 人民大道201号; ⏰9.30am-5pm; M People's Sq)

Shiatzy Chen
CLOTHING

Located around the corner from Sūzhōu Cobblers (see **23** 🔒 Map p34, G3), Taiwanese designer Shiatzy Chen is one of the top names in Asian haute couture, and finds her inspiration in traditional Chinese aesthetics. The exclusive collections (women's and men's apparel) at her Bund 9 flagship store display a painstaking attention to detail, gracefully crossing cultural boundaries. (夏姿; Xià Zī; 📞 021 6321 9155; 9 East Zhongshan No 1 Rd; 中山东一路9号; ⏰10am-10pm; M East Nanjing Rd)

Blue Shànghǎi White
CERAMICS

Just off the Bund, right near Sūzhōu Cobblers (see **23** 🔒 Map p34, G3), this little boutique is a great place to browse for a contemporary take on a traditional art form. It sells a tasteful selection of hand-painted porcelain teacups (from ¥150), teapots and vases, displayed together with the store's ingeniously designed wooden furniture. (海晨; Hǎi Chén; 📞 021 6352 2222; unit 103, 17 Fuzhou Rd; 福州路17号103室; ⏰10.30am-6.30pm; M East Nanjing Rd) ▸

Local Life
Hóngkǒu

Getting There

Hóngkǒu is located north of the Bund.

Ⓜ **Metro** North Sichuan Rd (line 10) is the closest station.

Originally the American Settlement and later the Japanese district, Hóngkǒu is decidedly hard-working today, with many residents originating from nearby provinces such as Ānhuī and Jiāngsū. It's somewhat run-down and grittier than other areas of Shànghǎi, but the lack of polish means there's plenty of interesting street life and creaky architecture waiting for discovery.

❶ Hongkew Methodist Church

This 1923 **church** (景灵堂; Jǐnglíng Táng; 135 Kunshan Rd; 昆山路135号) is where General Chiang Kaishek married Song Meiling (May-ling) in 1927. Meiling's father, Charlie, preached here briefly before he went into business as a printer. It's closed to the public, but the caretaker might let you in.

❷ Young Allen Court

West along Kunshan Rd on the corner with Zhapu Rd stands this distinctive brick **building** (260 Zhapu Rd; 乍浦路260号), constructed in 1923. Walk down the side of the alley for views of its three-storey architecture and the rear of the adjacent church towards the end.

❸ Shíkùmén Houses

This *lòng* (里弄; alley; No 13, the first on your left) doesn't look like anything special from the outside, but a wander down will reveal a row of eight decorative lintels, some of which are still fronted by the traditional black wooden doors of *shíkùmén* (石库门; stone-gate) homes.

❹ Art Deco Apartment Block

Near the intersection of Kunshan Rd and Baiguan St is a 1932 art deco apartment block. It stands adjacent to a line of grey-and-red-brick row houses, notable for their arched windows.

❺ Tanggu Road Food Market

Chinese markets always make for a fascinating stroll, though in Shànghǎi they can be hard to find, unless you know where to look. This reliable spot is open throughout the day; you'll find all manner of things for sale, including thousand-year-old eggs.

❻ North Jiangxi Road

This fun, buzzing strip has scooters pushing through crowds of pedestrians, while the street sides are lined with vendors selling fresh sugar-cane juice and snacks. The distinctive old house at No 174 was allegedly the residence of Lotus, a gangster–police inspector's concubine.

❼ Clothing Market

Qīpǔ Market (七浦服装市场; Qīpǔ Fúzhuāng Shìchǎng; 168 & 183 Qipu Rd; 七浦路168、183号; ⏱west side 5am-5pm, east side 7am-7pm; Ⓜ Tiantong Rd) is where the masses come shopping for clothes and shoes. Consisting of two warren-like department stores surrounding the North Henan Rd intersection, it's one big 'everything must go now' sale. Haggle hard.

❽ Shànghǎi Post Museum

The **Post Museum** (上海邮政博物馆, Shànghǎi Yóuzhèng Bówùguǎn; 2nd fl, 250 North Suzhou Rd; 苏州北路250号2楼; admission free; ⏱9am-5pm Wed, Thu, Sat & Sun, last entry 4pm; Ⓜ Tiantong Rd), where you can learn about Imperial China's postal history and view rare stamps, is intriguing. It's located in the magnificent British-built 1924 Post Office, capped with a baroque-style clock tower.

Explore

Old Town

Shànghǎi's Old Town, known to locals as Nán Shì (南市; Southern City), is an intriguing area of old-fashioned textures, tatty charm and musty temples, and is a favourite stop for visitors. The circular layout still reflects the footprint of the former city walls, flung up in the 16th century to defend against marauding Japanese pirates.

The Sights in a Day

☀ Pre-empt the crowds by arriving early at **Yùyuán Gardens & Bazaar** (p50). After visiting the gardens, exit into Yùyuán Bazaar and consider a cup of tea at the **Húxīntíng Teahouse** (p51) or a short wander amid the endless bustle of the market area. From here, find **Chénxiānggé Nunnery** (p52) and take a **walking tour** (p52) of the nearby temples, alleyways and antique markets. Break for lunch at **Nánxiáng Steamed Bun Restaurant** (p58) or **Sōngyuèlóu** (p58).

☼ Finish by browsing through the **Shíliùpù Fabric Market** (p53), which specialises in tailor-made clothing, then catch a taxi to the **Confucius Temple** (p55) and explore its surrounding alleyways, which are much less touristy than the area around the Yùyuán Bazaar. Continue to the **Flower, Bird, Fish & Insect Market** (p56).

☾ For dinner and drinks, head to East Nanjing Rd (and the Bund), one stop away on the metro from Yuyuan Garden station, or head to the riverside **Cool Docks** (p56).

For a local's day in the Old Town, see p52.

👁 Top Sights

Yùyuán Gardens & Bazaar (p50)

🔍 Local Life

Backstreets & Alleyways (p52)

💙 Best of Shànghǎi

Temples & Churches

Chénxiānggé Nunnery (p52)

Confucius Temple (p55)

Temple of the Town God (p51)

Markets & Antiques

Old Street (p53)

Shíliùpù Fabric Market (p53)

Fúyòu Antique Market (p53)

Eating

Nánxiáng Steamed Bun Restaurant (p58)

Sōngyuèlóu (p58)

Getting There

Ⓜ **Metro** Line 10 runs through the Old Town. Yuyuan Garden station is close to most sights.

🚲 **Pedicabs** Look for unofficial pedicabs in the streets leading off the Bund; a trip to Yùyuán Gardens costs around ¥10 (total, not per person).

Top Sights
Yùyuán Gardens & Bazaar

With their shaded alcoves, pavilions, glittering pools churning with carp, and pines sprouting wistfully from rockeries, the Yùyuán Gardens are one of Shànghǎi's premier sights – but they can be overpoweringly crowded at weekends. The surrounding streets and Buddhist and Taoist temples are among the few places in the city that retain a flavour of yesteryear, so if you're in need of an antidote to Shànghǎi's relentless quest for modernity, this is the place to come.

◉ Map p54, C2

豫园、豫园商城; Yùyuán & Yùyuán Shāngchéng

Anren Jie; 安仁街

low/high season ¥30/40

⏱8.30am-5.30pm, last entry at 5pm

Ⓜ Yuyuan Garden

Don't Miss

Origins

Founded between 1559 and 1577 by the well-to-do Pan family, these classical Chinese gardens are a fine example of Ming-dynasty design, although they were ransacked during both the Opium War and the Taiping Rebellion. The ingenious use of alcoves, windows and doorways lends an impression of size to a relatively small area.

Garden Highlights

Keep an eye out for the **Great Rockery** and **Sānsuì Hall**, two of the first sights you'll encounter upon entering the garden. Another curiosity is the **Exquisite Jade Rock**, which was bound for the imperial court in Běijīng until the boat sank off Shànghǎi. Also look for the **Hall of Heralding Spring**, which in 1853 was the headquarters for the Small Swords Society, and the beautiful **stage** (1888), with its gilded carved ceiling.

Yùyuán Bazaar

Surrounding the gardens is Yùyuán Bazaar, a bustling maze of souvenir stalls and famous snack shops. You'll spot plenty of fake Rolexes, but shopping here is nevertheless entertaining. Join the crowds surrounding the *lāyángpiān* (拉洋片; peephole theatre) performer and don't forget to haggle.

Temple of the Town God

Chinese towns traditionally had a community of Taoist gods (often presided over by a main town god), who kept the populace from harm. This **temple** (城隍庙; Chénghuáng Miào; Yùyuán Bazaar; admission ¥10; ☉8.30am-4.30pm; Ⓜ Yuyuan Garden), accessed from Middle Fangbang Rd, originally dated to the early 15th century but was badly damaged during the Cultural Revolution.

☑ Top Tips

► Classical Chinese gardens were not designed to accommodate more than 1000 visitors a day. For the best experience, make sure you get here at opening time, before the tour buses arrive.

► Pick up a map of the surrounding Yùyuán Bazaar at the **Tourist Information and Service Centre** (旅游咨询服务中心; Lǚyóu Zīxún Fúwù Zhōngxīn; ☎021 6355 5032; 149 Jiujiaochang Rd; 旧校场路149号; ☉9am-7pm), near the intersection with Old St.

✖ Take a Break

Next to the garden entrance is the **Húxīntíng Teahouse** (湖心亭茶楼; Húxīntíng Chálóu; tea upstairs/downstairs ¥50/35; ☉8.30am-9.30pm), once part of the gardens and now one of the most famous teahouses in China. Its zigzag causeway, which can confuse visitors, is designed to thwart evil spirits, who can only travel in straight lines.

Local Life
Backstreets & Alleyways

The Old Town is a fascinating place to wander, particularly because it is one of the last bastions of traditional life in Shànghǎi. Real-estate development encroaches on what remains of the neighbourhood, but sneak into a back alley and you can still get a glimpse of life as it was 60 years ago.

❶ Chénxiānggé Nunnery

Seek out the tidy floral courtyard at the rear of this delightful **temple** (沉香阁; Chénxiāng Gé; 29 Chenxiangge Rd; 沉香阁路29号; admission ¥10; ⊘7am-5pm; Ⓜ Yuyuan Garden), with its brown-clothed Buddhist nuns, to climb the **Guānyīn Tower** (观音楼; Guānyīn Lóu; admission ¥2; ⊘7am-3pm), housing an effigy of the goddess of mercy, carved from *chénxiāng* (沉香) wood and seated in *lalitasana* (seated half-lotus) posture.

❷ Wangyima Alley

Bypass the souvenir free-for-all outside the temple and follow this twisting alleyway. You'll still find pseudo antiques alongside the sizzle of woks and makeshift noodle stands, but the shops soon give way to doting grandparents and drying laundry. It's a veritable maze; look out for Zhongwang Yima Alley (中王医马弄; Zhōngwáng Yīmǎ Nòng) and turn right.

❸ Old Street

The morass of Mao-era keepsakes holds no surprises, but the ye-olde-China streetscape of **Old Street** (老街; Lǎo Jiē; Middle Fangbang Rd; 方浜中路; M Yuyuan Garden) – once a canal – is entertaining, with shops spilling forth shadow puppets, jade jewellery, embroidered fabrics, kites, chopsticks, yíxìng (宜兴) teapots, Tibetan jewellery and repro posters.

❹ Antique Hunting

There's a permanent antique market here on the 1st and 2nd floors, but the **Fúyòu Antique Market** (福佑工艺品市场; Fúyòu Gōngyìpǐn Shìchǎng; 459 Middle Fangbang Rd; 方浜中路459号; M Yuyuan Garden) really gets humming on the 'ghost market' on weekends, when sellers from the countryside fill up all four floors and then some. Mornings are best.

❺ Tea Time

The **Old Shànghǎi Teahouse** (老上海茶馆; Lǎo Shànghǎi Cháguǎn; ☏ 021 5382 1202; 385 Middle Fangbang Rd; 方浜中路385号; tea from ¥45; ⏰ 9am-9pm; M Yuyuan Garden) is much like someone's attic, where ancient gramophones, records, typewriters and other period clutter share space with the aroma of Chinese tea and tempting snacks.

❻ Return to the Alleyways

Pass the Temple of the Town God and then turn left to return to the Old Town's quiet alleyways, with their hanging laundry, bicycle bells and outdoor mah-jong games. Check out the lovely old doorways on Danfeng Rd, such as the carved red-brick gateway at No 193.

❼ Middle Fangbang Road

Note the old stone archway when you turn back onto Middle Fangbang Rd. These archways, known as *páilou* (牌楼) or *páifāng* (牌坊), originally marked the entrance to local communities within a larger neighbourhood. Middle Fangbang Rd remains a boisterous shopping street, filled with snack stands and booming stereo systems.

❽ Tailored Clothing

Head to the **Shíliùpù Fabric Market** (十六铺面料城; Shíliùpù Miànliào Chéng; ☏ 021 6330 1043; 2 Zhonghua Rd; 中华路2号; ⏰ 8.30am-6.30pm; M Xiaonanmen) to browse for inexpensive silk, cashmere, wool, linen and cotton, but check for quality. Tailored clothing is a steal – count on one to three days' turnaround.

0   500 m
0   0.25 miles

Ferry to Pudong

Huángpǔ River

E Zhongshan No 2 Rd 中山东二路

Yangshuo Rd 阳朔路
Zhonghua Rd 中华路

Cool Docks
S Zhongshan Rd

Maojiayuan Rd 毛家园路
Baidu Rd 白渡路
Dongjiadu Rd

E Fuxing Rd 复兴东路

Renmin Rd 人民路

Xinyongan Rd 新永安路

E Jinling Rd 金陵东路

Yùyuán Gardens & Bazaar

Anren St 安仁街

Wutong Rd 梧桐路
Sipailou Rd 四牌楼路
Zhoujin Rd 竹行路

Xueyuan Rd 学院路

Xiaonanmen
小南门站

Xundao St 巡道街

E Fuxing Rd 复兴东路

S Guangqi Rd

Wangyun Rd
望云路

S Henan Rd 河南南路

Huangjia Rd 黄家路
Shangwen Rd 尚文路
Zhonghua St 中华街

Jiujiaochang Rd 旧校场路

Fuyou Rd 福佑路
Middle Fangbang Rd 方浜中路

Yuyuan Garden 豫园站

E Yan'an Rd 延安东路

E Fujian Rd 福建南路
E Ningbo Rd 宁波东路
E Jinling Rd 金陵东路

Middle Henan Rd

S Henan Rd 河南南路
Changsheng St 长生街

W Fangbang Rd 方浜西路

Dajing Rd 大境路
Dajing Pavilion

Middle Fangbang Rd 方浜中路

Zhua Rd 竹行路

OLD TOWN (NÁNSHÌ)

E Fuxing Rd 复兴东路

Jingxiu Rd 静修路

Menghua St
Penglai Rd 蓬莱路
Xueqian St 学前街

Confucius Temple 文庙
Wenmiao Rd 文庙路

Daxing St 大兴街
Dajing Rd 大境路

S Henan Rd 河南南路

Laoximen
老西门站

S Xizang Rd

Dashijie 大世界站

S E Huaihai Rd 淮海东路

Renmin Rd 人民路

S Xizang Rd

Shouning Rd 寿宁路

Hubin Rd 湖滨路

Zizhong Rd 自忠路

Liulin Rd

Flower, Bird, Fish & Insect Market

Huiji Rd 会稽路

Middle Fuxing Rd 复兴中路

Hefei Rd 合肥路

E Jianguo Rd

PŬXĪ

Zhonghua St 中华街
Daji Rd 大吉路

Confucius Temple

Sights

Confucius Temple TEMPLE

1 Map p54, B4

A modest and charming retreat, this well-tended temple to Confucius is cultivated with maples, pines, magnolias and birdsong. The layout is typically Confucian, its few worshippers complemented by ancient and venerable trees, including a 300-year-old elm. The main hall for worshipping Confucius is **Dàchéng Hall** (大成殿; Dàchéng Diàn), complete with twin eaves and a statue of the sage outside. (文庙; Wén Miào; 215 Wenmiao Rd; 文庙路215号; adult/student ¥10/5; ☺9am-5pm, last entry 4.30pm; MLaoximen)

Dàjìng Pavilion HISTORIC SITE

2 Map p54, A2

Dating from 1815, this pavilion contains the only preserved section of the 5km-long city walls. Also within the pavilion is a small Guandi temple, which found a new calling as a factory during the Cultural Revolution. In the middle sits the fiery-faced Guandi, with an equally fierce God of Wealth to his left and Yuexia Laoren (月下老人) to his right. (大境阁; Dàjìng Gé; 259 Dajing Rd; 大境路; admission ¥5; ☺9am-4pm; MDashijie)

Cool Docks

ARCHITECTURE

3 🎯 Map p54, E3

The riverside Cool Docks consist of several *shíkùmén* (石库门; stone-gate houses) surrounded by red-brick warehouses, near (but not quite on) the waterfront. Now full of restaurants and bars and all lit up at night, the Cool Docks' isolated position (it lacks the central location and transport connections of Xīntiāndì in the French Concession) has hobbled ambitions. Although high-profile and trendy restaurant, bar and hotel openings have helped give it a much-needed lift, it remains an entertainment backwater. (老码头; www.thecooldocks.com; 479 South Zhongshan Rd; 中山南路479号; **M**Xiaonanmen)

Flower, Bird, Fish & Insect Market

MARKET

4 🎯 Map p54, A3

One of few remaining traditional markets in town, this spot is a fascinating experience. Wander among the racket of crickets, interlaced with snatches of birdsong, to a backdrop of multicoloured fish flitting about. Crickets come in a variety of sizes and are sold in woven bamboo cages for under ¥30. (万商花鸟鱼虫市场; Wànshāng Huā Niǎo Yú Chóng Shìchǎng; South Xizang Rd; 西藏南路; **M**Laoximen)

LONELY PLANET / GETTY IMAGES ©

Flower, Bird, Fish & Insect Market

Understand

Guanyin

Encountered in Buddhist temples across Shànghǎi and China, the bodhisattva Guanyin is the Buddhist Goddess of Mercy. Her full name is Guanshiyin (观世音; literally, 'Observing the Cries of the World'), but she is also called Guanzizai, Guanyin Dashi and Guanyin Pusa, or, in Sanskrit, Avalokiteshvara. Known as Kannon in Japanese, Guanyam in Cantonese and Quan Am in Vietnamese, she is one of the most recognisable figures in Buddhism. Her mission is to offer sympathy to the world, from a wellspring of infinite compassion, and she is most revered by female worshippers.

Finding the Goddess

Guanyin can often be found at the very rear of the main hall, facing north (most of the other divinities, apart from Weituo, face south). She typically has her own little shrine and stands on the head of a big fish, holding a lotus in her hand, with attendant *luóhàn* (罗汉; arhats) and children on a montage behind her. On other occasions, she has her own hall, often towards the rear of the temple (as in Chénxiānggé Nunnery in the Old Town; p52). Sometimes, she is worshipped within her very own temple.

Her Manifestations

In ancient Chinese effigies, the goddess was male rather than female and can sometimes be found seated lalitasana, a lithe and relaxed regal posture where one of Guanyin's feet typically rests on, or near, the thigh of the other leg.

Guanyin can appear in many forms, often with just two arms, but sometimes in a multiarmed form or with a fan of arms behind her in the famous 1000-hand form (Qiānshǒu Guānyīn). The 11-faced Guanyin, the fierce horse-head Guanyin, the Songzi Guanyin (literally 'Offering Son Guanyin') and the Dripping Water Guanyin are just some of her myriad manifestations. She was also a favourite subject for *déhuà* (德化) glazed porcelain figures, which are very elegant and either snow-white or creamy. Examples exist in the Shànghǎi Museum (p28).

Eating

Nánxiáng Steamed Bun Restaurant
DUMPLING $

5 Map p54, C2

Shànghǎi's most famous dumpling restaurant divides the purists, who love the place, from the younger crowd, who see an overrated tourist trap. Decide for yourself how the *xiǎolóngbāo* rate, but lines are long and you won't even get near it on weekends. There are three dining halls upstairs, with the prices escalating (and crowds diminishing) in each room. (南翔馒头店; Nánxiáng Mántou Diàn; 85 Yuyuan Rd, Yùyuán Bazaar; 豫园商城豫园路85号; 1st fl per 16 dumplings ¥20; ⏰1st fl 10am-9pm, 2nd fl 7am-8pm, 3rd fl 9.30am-7pm; Ⓜ Yuyuan Garden)

Sōngyuèlóu
CHINESE $

6 Map p54, C2

Dating to 1910, this place has decent-value vegie cheap eats such as wonton (馄饨汤; *húntún tāng*; ¥10), and tofu masquerading as meat such as black-pepper beef noodle soup (¥35). Upstairs has an English menu, spotless tablecloths and a price hike. Downstairs is a busy, Mandarin-only canteen-style affair where you order first, get a receipt and share tables. (松月楼; ☏021 6355 3630; 23 Bailing Rd; 百灵路23号; dishes from ¥10; ⏰7am-7.30pm; ✎🗊; Ⓜ Yuyuan Garden)

Drinking

Char Bar
BAR

7 Ⓨ Map p54, D2

One of Shànghǎi's supreme al fresco bars, Char Bar is tops for cocktails while neon-gazing. The terrace boasts some of the finest views over the Bund, the Huángpǔ River and Pǔdōng, while inside it's chill and hip. From 8.30pm Thursday to Saturday, there's a ¥100 cover charge (including one drink). Drinks cost ¥50 between 5pm and 8.30pm Monday to Thursday. (恰酒吧; Qià Jiǔbā; www.char-thebund.com; 30th fl, Hotel Indigo, 585 East Zhongshan No 2 Rd; 中山东二路585号30楼; ⏰5pm-1.30am Mon-Thu, to 2.30am Fri & Sat, 2pm-1am Sun; Ⓜ Xiaonanmen)

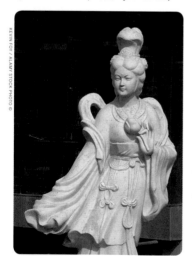

KEVIN FOY / ALAMY STOCK PHOTO ©

Statue in the Yùyuán Gardens (p50)

Dàjìng Pavilion (p55)

Shopping

South Bund Fabric Market

FABRIC

8 🔒 Map p54, D4

This old building with more than 100 stalls has an atmospheric location not far from the markets and tailoring shops along Dongjiadu Rd. It's a bit out of the way, but popular with expats. (南外滩轻纺面料市场; Nán Wàitān Qīngfǎng Miànliào Shìchǎng; 399 Lujiabang Rd; 陆家浜路399号; ⏱8.30am-6pm; Ⓜ Nanpu Bridge)

Tóng Hán Chūn Traditional Medicine Store

CHINESE MEDICINE

9 🔒 Map p54, C2

An intriguing emporium of elixirs, infusions and remedies, this place has been selling Chinese medicinal cures since 1783. There's a vast range here, including modern medications, but it's all labelled in Chinese and little English is spoken, so take along a translator. On the 3rd floor, traditional Chinese medicine (TCM) doctors offer consultations (you'll need an appointment). (童涵春堂; Tóng Hán Chūn Táng; 📞 021 6355 0308; 20 New Yuyuan Rd; 上海豫园新路20号; ⏱8am-9pm; Ⓜ Yuyuan Garden)

Explore

French Concession East

For full immersion in Shànghǎi's most chic and fashionable charms, there's little need to stray from the French Concession. Once home to the lion's share of Shànghǎi's adventurers, radicals, gangsters, writers, prostitutes and pimps, the area's tree-lined streets and European villas were where Shànghǎi's very reputation as the 'Paris of the East' was nurtured.

The Sights in a Day

☼ The French Concession doesn't really get going until 10am at the earliest. Begin the day at **Xīntiāndì** (p64), where you can explore the **Shíkùmén Open House Museum** (p65) and stroll the prettified alleyways while boutique hunting. Scout out Xīntiāndì's fabulous collection of restaurants as you go – **Xīnjíshì** (p71) and **Crystal Jade** (p71) are two favourites.

☼ Follow the **walking tour** (p118) to get a feel for the Concession's backstreets, shopping strips and historic architecture. Afterwards, head to **Tiánzǐfáng** (p62) to check out the **Liúli China Museum** (p63) and assorted galleries before they close for the day, and then it's on to a second round of boutique hopping – or perhaps you'd prefer to celebrate happy hour on Yongkang Rd at the **Café des Stagiaires** (p72).

☾ Evenings are ripe with promise. There's no shortage of great restaurants, such as **Dī Shuǐ Dòng** (p70) or **Cha's** (p70), which you can follow up with a **massage** (p131) or perhaps a concert at **MAO Livehouse** (p74).

◉ Top Sights
Tiánzǐfáng (p62)

Xīntiāndì (p64)

♥ Best of Shànghǎi

Eating

Dī Shuǐ Dòng (p70)

Din Tai Fung (p70)

Cha's (p70)

Crystal Jade (p71)

T8 (p70)

Yè Shànghǎi (p72)

Boutiques

Tiánzǐfáng (p62)

Xīntiāndì (p74)

Heirloom (p74)

Yúnwúxīn (p74)

Shanghai Tang (p74)

Getting There

Ⓜ **Metro** Lines 1 and 10 serve the area, both running east–west past Xīntiāndì. Line 1 continues on to People's Square, while line 10 serves the Old Town and East Nanjing Rd (the Bund). The two lines meet at the South Shaanxi Rd metro stop. At the southern edge of the concession is line 9, serving Tiánzǐfáng.

Top Sights
Tiánzǐfáng

Xīntiāndì and Tiánzǐfáng are based on a similar idea – a retail complex housed within a layout of traditional *lòngtáng* (弄堂; alleyways) – but when it comes to genuine charm and vibrancy, Tiánzǐfáng is the one that delivers. A community of design studios, local families, wi-fi cafes and start-up boutiques, it's the perfect antidote to Shànghǎi's oversized malls and intimidating skyscrapers, but it's frequently crammed with visitors.

Map p66, E5

www.tianzifang.cn

田子坊

Taikang Rd; 泰康路

M Dapuqiao

A shop selling cuttlefish in Tiánzǐfáng

Don't Miss

Shopping

Burrow into the *lǐlòng* (里弄; alleys) here for a rewarding haul of creative boutiques, selling everything from hip jewellery and vintage fashion to nifty artwork. Standout stores include **Shànghǎi 1936** (Unit 110, No 3, Lane 210) for tailored clothes, **Pilingpalang** (No 220, Lane 210) for funky ceramics and cloisonné, vintage spectacles at **Shànghǎi Code** (No 9, Lane 274), and the eye-catching books, notepads, posters and art of **Link Shànghǎi** (No 5, Lane 248).

Liúli China Museum

Located across the way from Tiánzǐfáng, this **museum** (琉璃艺术博物馆; Liúli Yìshù Bówùguǎn; www.liulichinamuseum.com; 25 Taikang Rd; admission ¥20; ⏰10am-5pm; Ⓜ Dapuqiao) is dedicated to the art of glass sculpture (*pâte de verre* or lost-wax casting). Peruse the collection of ancient Chinese artefacts, contemporary creations and the founders' own sublime Buddhist-inspired pieces. A giant steel peony adorns the building's exterior.

Lòngtáng

As you plunge into Tiánzǐfáng, you'll find yourself in a delightful – but crowded – web of *lòngtáng* (alleyways) and *shíkùmén* houses. While browsing, and dodging the crowds, it's easy to miss the traditional buildings around you, but it's the architecture and layout that make Tiánzǐfáng tick and lend the zone its charming grid-like structure.

Bars & Cafes

There are several great bars and cafes hidden in the alleyways here, but you may have to spend some time looking for the best places. Top picks include **Kommune** (公社; Gōngshè; The Yard, No 7, Lane 210, Taikang Rd; meals from ¥68; ⏰7am-1am), **Kāibā** (开巴; www.kaiba-beerbar.com; 2nd fl, 169 Middle Jianguo Rd; ⏰11am-2am) and Bell Bar (p73).

☑ Top Tips

▶ Tiánzǐfáng consists of three main north–south lanes (Nos 210, 248 and 274) crisscrossed by irregular east–west alleyways, which makes exploration slightly disorienting, but fun. Some addresses use Middle Jianguo Rd, which runs parallel to Taikang Rd and serves as the north entrance.

▶ Shops here generally open from 10am to 8pm.

▶ Although there are plenty of dining options, there is no Chinese cuisine. You'll most likely have to decide between cafe fare, Thai and pizza.

✗ Take a Break

Bell Bar (p73) is a charmingly offbeat spot for taking the weight off your feet, sitting back with a good read and raising a glass in boho surrounds.

Top Sights
Xīntiāndì

With its own namesake metro station, Xīntiāndì has been a Shànghǎi icon for a decade or more. An upscale entertainment complex modelled on traditional *lòngtáng* homes, this was the first development in the city to prove that historic architecture makes big commercial sense. Elsewhere that might sound like a no-brainer, but in the first years of 21st-century China, where bulldozers were always on standby, it came as quite a revelation.

◉ Map p66, F2

www.xintiandi.com

新天地

2 blocks between Taicang, Zizhong, Madang & South Huangpi Rds; 太仓路与马当路路口

Ⓜ South Huangpi Rd, Xintiandi

TMSK bar

Don't Miss

Shíkùmén Open House Museum

This invitingly restored two-storey **stone-gate house** (石库门屋里厢; Shíkùmén Wūlǐxiāng; Xīntiāndì North Block, Bldg 25; 太仓路181弄新天地北里25号楼; adult/child ¥20/10; ⏱10.30am-10.30pm; Ⓜ South Huangpi Rd, Xintiandi) is decorated with period furniture and infused with the charms of historical Shànghǎi. Peek into the minute, wedge-shaped *tíngzǐjiān* (亭子间) room, which used to be rented out to cash-strapped writers and other penurious tenants.

Dining

The drinking and dining venues are wedged in cheek by jowl and are the essence of Xīntiāndì. You can find plenty of coffee and comfort food if that's what you're after, but don't overlook the superb Shanghainese options such as Xīnjíshì (p71) and Yè Shànghǎi (p72). For dumplings and dim sum, head to Din Tai Fung (p70) or Crystal Jade (p71).

Shopping

Window shoppers can make a fun afternoon of it here. See p74 for selected stores.

Site of the 1st National Congress of the CCP

The communist back-slapping might grate with some visitors, but this lovely *shíkùmén* house (中共一大会址纪念馆; Zhōnggòng Yīdàhuìzhǐ Jìniànguǎn; Xīntiāndì North Block, 76 Xingye Rd; 兴业路76号; admission free; ⏱9am-5pm; Ⓜ South Huangpi Rd, Xintiandi) is immortalised as one of China's holiest political shrines, where the Chinese Communist Party (CCP) was founded on 23 July 1921. Bring your passport.

☑ Top Tips

▶ The first mall holds three top-notch restaurants on the 2nd floor; Din Tai Fung (p70), Crystal Jade (p71) and **Shànghǎi Min** (小南国; Xiǎo Nán Guó; ☎400 820 9777; Xīntiāndì South Block, 2nd fl, Bldg 6; 兴业路123弄新天地南里6号楼2楼; dishes ¥38-158; 🖥; Ⓜ South Huangpi Rd, Xintiandi), while Xīntiāndì Style mall showcases local brands and chic clothes.

▶ Apart from two worthwhile sights – Shíkùmén Open House Museum and the Site of the 1st National Congress of the CCP – strolling the prettified alleyways and enjoying an evening drink or a meal is the best approach.

✕ Take a Break

Worth a visit as much for the decor as for the drinks, **TMSK** (透明思考; Tòumíng Sīkǎo; ☎021 6326 2227; Xīntiāndì North Block, Bldg 11; 太仓路181弄新天地北里11号楼; ⏱11.30am-1am; 📶; Ⓜ South Huangpi Rd, Xintiandi) is designed to within an inch of its life.

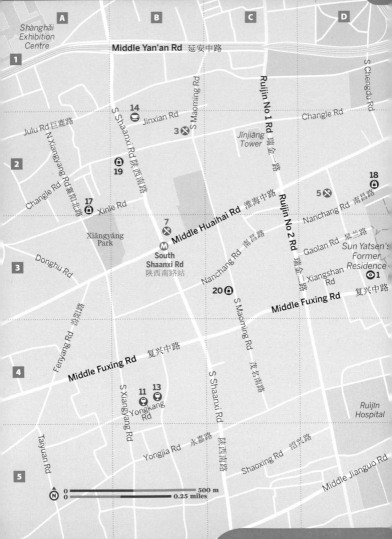

Shànghǎi Exhibition Centre

Middle Yan'an Rd 延安中路

Julu Rd 巨鹿路

N Xiangyang Rd 襄阳北路

Changle Rd

S Shaanxi Rd 陕西南路

Jinxian Rd

14

S Maoming Rd

3

Ruijin No 1 Rd 瑞金一路

Changle Rd

Jīnjiāng Tower

19

Xinle Rd

17

18

Nanchang Rd 南昌路

5

Ruijin No 2 Rd 瑞金二路

Xiāngyáng Park

7

Middle Huaihai Rd 淮海中路

Nanchang Rd 南昌路

Gaolan Rd 皋兰路

Sun Yatsen's Former Residence

Donghu Rd

Ⓜ South Shaanxi Rd 陕西南路站

Nanchang Rd 南昌路

Xiangshan Rd

1

20

S Maoming Rd

Ruijin No 2 Rd 瑞金二路

Middle Fuxing Rd 复兴中路

Fenyang Rd 汾阳路

Middle Fuxing Rd 复兴中路

S Shaanxi Rd 陕西南路

S Maoming Rd 茂名南路

Ruìjīn Hospital

S Xiangyang Rd

11 **13**

Yongkang Rd

Taiyuan Rd

Yongjia Rd 永嘉路

S Shaanxi Rd 陕西南路

Shaoxing Rd 绍兴路

Middle Jianguo Rd

N ⊕ 0 ───────── 500 m
0 ───────── 0.25 miles

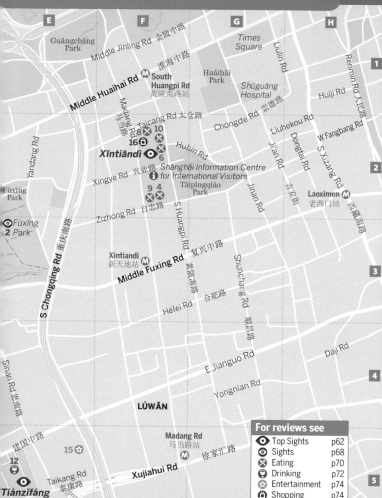

Guǎngchǎng Park

Middle Jinling Rd 金陵中路

淮海中路

Times Square

Middle Huaihai Rd

South Huangpi Rd 黄陂南路站

Huáihǎi Park

Liulin Rd

Renmin Rd 人民路

Yandang Rd

Madang Rd 马当路

Taicang Rd 太仓路

8 ✕ **10** ✕
16 🔒 ✕

Chongde Rd 崇德路

Shǔguāng Hospital

Huiji Rd

W Fangbang Rd

S Xizang Rd

Liuhekou Rd

Xīntiāndì ◉ ✕ **6**

Hubin Rd

Shànghǎi Information Centre for International Visitors ℹ

Dongtai Rd

Fùxīng Park

Xingye Rd 兴业路

9 ✕ **4** ✕

Tàipíngqiáo Park

Jian Rd

Jinan Rd

Laoximen Ⓜ 老西门站

S Chongqing Rd 重庆南路

◉ **Fùxīng 2 Park**

Zizhong Rd 自忠路

S Huangpi Rd

复兴中路

Xintiandi Ⓜ 新天地站
Middle Fuxing Rd

Shunchang Rd

Hefei Rd 合肥路

Sinan Rd 思南路

E Jianguo Rd

Daji Rd

Yongnian Rd

LÚWĀN

Madang Rd Ⓜ 马当路站

15 ✦

12 ◉

Tiánzǐfáng

Taikang Rd 泰康路

Xujiahui Rd 徐家汇路

Ⓜ **Dapuqiao** 打浦桥站

For reviews see	
◉ Top Sights	p62
◉ Sights	p68
✕ Eating	p70
✕ Drinking	p72
✦ Entertainment	p74
🔒 Shopping	p74

JOHN NORMAN / ALAMY STOCK PHOTO ©

Women in Fùxīng Park

Sights

Sun Yatsen's
Former Residence   HISTORIC BUILDING

1 🎯 Map p66, D3

Sun Zhongshan predictably receives
the full-on hagiographic treatment
at this shrine to China's *guófù* (国父;
father of the nation). A capacious exhibition hall next door further pampers
his memory and serves as an intense
prelude to his pebble-dash 'Spanish-style' home. (孙中山故居; Sūn Zhōngshān
Gùjū; 7 Xiangshan Rd; 香山路7号; admission
¥20; audio guide ¥30; ⏰9am-4pm; Ⓜ South
Shaanxi Rd, Xintiandi)

Fùxīng Park   PARK

2 🎯 Map p66, E3

This leafy spot with a large lawn, laid
out by the French in 1909 and later
used by the Japanese as a parade
ground in the late 1930s, remains
one of the city's more enticing parks.
There is always plenty to see here:
the park is a refuge for the elderly
and a practising field for itinerant
musicians, chess players, people
walking backwards and slow-moving
taichi types. (复兴公园; Fùxīng Gōngyuán;
⏰5am-6pm; Ⓜ South Shaanxi Rd, Xintiandi)

Understand

Green Gang Gangsters

In Shànghǎi's climate of hedonistic freedoms, political ambiguities and capitalist free-for-all, it was perhaps inevitable that the city should spawn China's most powerful mobsters. Ironically, in 1930s Shànghǎi the most binding laws were those of the underworld, with its blood oaths, secret signals and strict code of honour. China's modern-day Triads and Snakeheads owe much of their form to their Shanghainese predecessors.

From Godfather...

The godfather of the Shànghǎi underworld was Du Yuesheng, or 'Big-Eared' Du as he was known to anyone brave enough to say it to his face. Born in Pǔdōng, Du soon moved across the river and was recruited into the Green Gang (青帮; Qīngbāng), where he worked for 'Pockmarked' Huang, a legendary gangster who doubled as a high-ranking detective in the French Concession police. Du gained fame by setting up an early opium cartel with the rival Red Gang and rising through the ranks. By 1927 Du was the head of the Green Gang and in control of the city's prostitution, drug-running, protection and labour rackets. His forte was to kidnap the rich and negotiate their release, taking half of the ransom money as commission. With an estimated 20,000 men at his beck and call, Du travelled in a bullet-proof sedan, protected by armed bodyguards crouched on the running boards.

His control of the labour rackets led to contacts with warlords and politicians. In 1927 Du played a major part in Chiang Kaishek's anti-communist massacre and later became an adviser to the Kuomintang. A fervent nationalist, he funded the anti-Japanese resistance movement.

...to Du-Gooder?

Strangely, Du always seemed to crave respectability. In 1931 he was elected to the Municipal Council and was known for years as the unofficial mayor of Shànghǎi. He became a Christian halfway through his life and somehow ended up best known as a philanthropist. When British poet WH Auden interviewed him in Shànghǎi in 1937, Du was head of the Chinese Red Cross!

During the Japanese occupation of Shànghǎi, Du fled to the city of Chóngqìng (Chungking). After the war he settled in Hong Kong, where he died, a multimillionaire, in 1951.

Eating

Dī Shuǐ Dòng
HUNANESE $$

3 🍴 Map p66, B2

Until the chilled lagers arrive, the faint breeze from the spreading of the blue-and-white tablecloth by your waiter may be the last cooling sensation at Dī Shuǐ Dòng, a rustic upstairs shrine to the volcanic cuisine of Húnán. Loved by Shanghainese and expats alike, dishes are ferried in by sprightly peasant-attired staff to tables stuffed with enthusiastic, red-faced diners. (滴水洞; 📞 021 6253 2689; 2nd fl, 56 South Maoming Rd; 茂名南路56号2楼; dishes ¥28-128; ⏰ 11am-12.30am; 🚇; 🚇 South Shaanxi Rd)

Din Tai Fung
DUMPLING $$

4 🍴 Map p66, F2

Scrummy dumplings – with a price tag – and classy service from Taiwan's most famous chain. It's on the 2nd floor, inside the Xīntiāndì mall. Reserve. (鼎泰丰; Dīng Tài Fēng; 📞 021 6385 8378; Xīntiāndì South Block, 2nd fl, Bldg 6; 兴业路123弄新天地南里6号楼2楼; 10 dumplings ¥60-96; ⏰ 10am-midnight; 🚇; 🚇 South Huangpi Rd, Xintiandi)

Cha's
CANTONESE $

5 🍴 Map p66, D2

This rammed Cantonese diner does its best to teleport you to 1950s Hong Kong, with old-style tiled floors, whirring ceiling fans and even an antique Coca-Cola ice box to set the scene. You'll need to wait to get a table, so use the time wisely and peruse the menu of classic comfort food (curries, sweet-and-sour pork) in advance. (查餐厅; Chá Cāntīng; 30 Sinan Rd; 思南路30号; dishes ¥20-55; ⏰ 11am-1.30am; 🚇 South Shaanxi Rd)

T8
FUSION $$$

6 🍴 Map p66, F2

T8 aims to seduce, which it does exceptionally well. Catalan chef Jordi Servalls Bonilla is at the helm, bringing a preference for molecular cuisine, with dishes such as watermelon salad 2.0, *tataki* of sesame-crusted tuna and Sìchuān high pie. The renovated grey-brick *shíkùmén* with a striking feng shui–driven entrance is the perfect setting. (📞 021 6355 8999; http://t8shanghai.com; Xīntiāndì North Block, Bldg 8; 太仓路181弄新天地北里8号楼; set lunch weekdays ¥168, 2-/3-course lunch weekends ¥258/328; ⏰ 11.30am-2pm & 6.30-11.30pm; 🚇; 🚇 South Huangpi Rd, Xintiandi)

Food Fusion
MALAYSIAN $$

7 🍴 Map p66, B3

Up on the 8th floor of one of Huaihai Rd's numerous shopping malls you'll find this hopping Malaysian option. Join the thronging office workers filling the lift and ascend to aromas of coriander, star anise, nutmeg, cinnamon and ginger. Crowd-pleasing classics include *rendang* beef, chilli-flecked *laksa* (coconut-curry noodle soup), chicken satay, fish curry, *roti canai* and Nyonya desserts. (融合; Rónghé; 8th fl, Parkson Plaza, 918 Middle Huaihai Rd; 淮海中路918号百盛8楼; dishes ¥30-168, lunch sets from ¥38; ⏰10am-11pm; 📶; Ⓜ South Shaanxi Rd)

Xīnjíshì
SHANGHAINESE $$

8 🍴 Map p66, F2

The Xīntiāndì branch of the classic Shanghainese restaurant Jesse. (新吉士; 📞021 6336 4746; Xīntiāndì North Block, Bldg 9; 新天地北里9号楼; dishes ¥40-88; ⏰11am-2pm & 5-9.30pm; Ⓜ South Huangpi Rd, Xintiandi)

Crystal Jade
DIM SUM $$

9 🍴 Map p66, F2

One of Xīntiāndì's long-standing success stories, Crystal Jade still draws lines out the door. What separates it from other dim-sum restaurants is the dough: dumpling skins are perfectly tender; steamed buns come out light and airy; and the freshly pulled noodles are just plain delicious. Go for lunch, when both Cantonese and Shanghainese dim sum are served. (翡翠酒家; Fěicuì Jiǔjiā; 📞021 6385 8752; Xīntiāndì South Block, 2nd fl, Bldg 6; 兴业路123弄新天地南里6号楼2楼; dim sum ¥20-42; ⏰11am-10.20pm; 📶; Ⓜ South Huangpi Rd, Xintiandi)

MICHAEL FREEMAN / CORBIS ©

Xīnjíshì

Taikang Road in Tiánzǐfáng (p62)

Yè Shànghǎi

SHANGHAINESE $$

10 Map p66, F2

Yè offers sophisticated, unchallenging Shanghainese cuisine in classy Xīntiāndì surroundings. The drunken-chicken and smoked-fish starters are an excellent overture to local flavours; the crispy duck comes with thick pancakes and the dish of sautéed string beans and bamboo shoots doesn't disappoint either. An affordable wine list gives it a further tick. (夜上海; ☎021 6311 2323; Xīntiāndì North Block, 338 South Huangpi Rd; 黄陂南路338号新天地北里; dishes ¥40-88, set lunch menu ¥68-88; ⓧ11.30am-2.30pm & 5.30-10.30pm; ⓪; Ⓜ South Huangpi Rd, Xintiandi)

Drinking

Café des Stagiaires

BAR

11 Map p66, B4

The best bar by far on buzzing Yongkang Rd, this hip oasis of Francophilia spills over with slightly zany Gallic charm. There's a Coke-bottle chandelier and a (French) geography lesson via the wine list: Languedoc, Provence, Côte du Rhône, Loire, Alsace, Bourgogne, Bordeaux and, *bien sûr*, Rest of the World. Each table is regularly stocked with addictive chilli peanuts. (www.cafestagiaires.com; 54-56 Yongkang Rd; 永康路54-56号; mains from ¥40; ⓧ10am-midnight; ⓐ; Ⓜ South Shaanxi Rd)

Bell Bar   BAR

12   Map p66, E5

This eccentric, unconventional boho haven is a delightful Tiánzǐfáng hideaway, with creaking, narrow wooden stairs leading to a higgledy-piggledy array of rooms to the tucked-away attic slung out above. Expect hookah pipes, mismatched furniture, warped secondhand paperbacks and a small, secluded mezzanine for stowaways from the bedlam outside. It's in the second alley (Lane 248) on the right. (bellbar.cn; Tiánzǐfáng, back door No 11, Lane 248, Taikang Rd; 泰康路248弄11号后门田子坊; ☻11am-2am; 🛜; MDapuqiao)

Dean's Bottle Shop   BAR

13   Map p66, B4

This well-priced nirvana for lovers of the grain (and, to a lesser extent, grape) has row upon row of imported bottled bliss – Moosehead lager, Old Rasputin, Young's double chocolate, Bombadier ale, pear cider – all at bargain prices. With more than enough labels to test even the most well-travelled palates, it's more shop than bar, but you can sit down. (40 Yongkang Rd; 永康路40号; beers from ¥15; ☻noon-10pm; MSouth Shaanxi Rd)

Citizen Café   CAFE

14   Map p66, B2

Decked out with small lampshades and panelled walls like a private living room, this is a quiet spot, and candlelit come sundown, when smooth, ambient sounds manage a relaxed tempo. Recharge with a club sandwich or sit back with one of the much-loved ginger cocktails while watching street scenes from the 2nd-floor terrace. Smokers sit by the door. (天台餐厅; Tiāntái Cāntīng; 222 Jinxian Rd; 进贤路222号; ☻11am-12.30am; 🛜; MSouth Shaanxi Rd)

Local Life
Yongkang Road Bar Street

A new bar street formed largely overnight during 2013 in the French Concession, kicked off by the peerless **Café des Stagiaires**, which still leads the way.

The small strip of Yongkang Rd between South Xiangyang Rd and Jiashan Rd was suddenly crammed with bars, making it a convenient catch-all similar to Hong Kong's Lan Kwai Fong entertainment area (albeit much smaller and quieter) for a night on the Shànghǎi tiles.

A pavement curfew at 10pm reigns, however, to appease locals living on the road, who were up in arms over the sudden, noisy transformation of their neighbourhood.

Entertainment

MAO Livehouse
LIVE MUSIC

15 ⭐ Map p66, E5

One of the city's best and largest music venues, MAO is a stalwart of the Shànghǎi music scene, with acts ranging from rock to pop to electronica. Check the website for schedules and ticket prices. (www.mao-music.com; 3rd fl, 308 South Chongqing Rd; 重庆南路308号3楼; Ⓜ Dapuqiao)

Shopping

Xīntiāndì
CLOTHING, ACCESSORIES

16 🔒 Map p66, F2

There are few bargains to be had at Xīntiāndì, but even window-shoppers can make a fun afternoon of it here. The North Block features embroidered accessories at **Annabel Lee** (安梨家居; Ānlí Jiājū; Xīntiāndì North Block, Bldg 3; 太仓路181弄新天地北里3号楼; ⏱10.30am-10.30pm; Ⓜ South Huangpi Rd, Xintiandi), high-end fashion from **Shanghai Tang** (上海滩; Shànghǎi Tān; Xīntiāndì North Block, Bldg 15; 太仓路181弄新天地北里15号楼; Ⓜ South Huangpi Rd) home furnishings at **Simply Life** (逸居生活; Yìjū Shēnghuó; ☎021 6387 5100;

Xīntiāndì North Block, Unit 101, 159 Madang Rd; 马当路159号新天地北里101单元; ⏱10.30am-10pm; Ⓜ South Huangpi Rd, Xintiandi) and a few scattered souvenir shops. The South Block has not one but two malls, including **Xīntiāndì Style** (新天地时尚; Xīntiāndì Shíshàng; 245 Madang Rd; 马当路245号). (新天地; www.xintiandi.com; 2 blocks btwn Taicang, Zizhong, Madang & South Huangpi Rds; 太仓路与马当路路口; Ⓜ South Huangpi Rd, Xintiandi)

Heirloom
ACCESSORIES

17 🔒 Map p66, A2

Heirloom's staple is a range of eye-catching, vibrant and stylish clutches, satchels and handbags, as well as smaller accessories such as leather wallets and bracelets. Prices range from ¥195 for a coin purse to around ¥4000. (78 Xinle Rd; 新乐路78号; ⏱10.30am-10pm; Ⓜ South Shaanxi Rd)

Yúnwúxīn
JEWELLERY

18 🔒 Map p66, D2

Drop by this incense-filled boutique to peruse the collection of handmade Tibetan-themed jewellery, fashioned from mother-of-pearl, red coral and turquoise. (云无心; 142 Nanchang Rd; 南昌路142号; ⏱11am-9pm; Ⓜ South Shaanxi Rd)

KARL JOHAENTGES / LOOK-FOTO / GETTY IMAGES ©

Shanghai Tang at Xīntiāndì

Garden Books

BOOKS

19 ⓐ Map p66, B2

The ice-cream parlour occupies about as much space as its well-stocked bookshelves. For all those Penguin paperback, gelato-to-go moments. (韬奋西文书局; Tāofèn Xīwén Shūjú; 325 Changle Rd; 长乐路325号; ⊘10am-10pm; 🛜; Ⓜ South Shaanxi Rd)

Huìfēng Tea Shop

TEA

20 ⓐ Map p66, C3

A friendly, reliable tea shop, which has good-quality clay teapots, cups and a great range of Chinese tea. Sample varieties and make your choice, or try 50g of Iron Guanyin (铁观音) for ¥20. (汇丰茶庄; Huìfēng Cházhuāng; ☎021 6472 7196; 124 South Maoming Rd; 茂名南路124号; ⊘9am-9.30pm; Ⓜ South Shaanxi Rd)

Explore

French Concession West

The French Concession's western half is an elegant treasure trove of art deco architecture, concession-era villas and atmospheric back-streets. As with the eastern half, shopping, drinking and dining are a visitor's most natural inclinations here. The district is not strong on individual sights, but its attractive streetscapes and inviting tempo make it one of the most stimulating and alluring parts of town.

The Sights in a Day

 Like the eastern half of the French Concession, the west sleeps late, so there's no need for an early start to the day. Two sights that are open in the morning include the **Propaganda Poster Art Centre** (p81) and the **Shànghǎi Arts & Crafts Museum** (p81). Lunch is a short taxi hop away: **Jian Guo 328** (p83) and **Noodle Bull** (p84) are two of the many fantastic options in the area.

 The numerous boutiques nearby – such as **Lolo Love Vintage** (p88) and **OOAK Concept Boutique** (p88) – will keep you dallying in the neighbourhood after lunch, but don't wait too long to explore the **concession-era architecture** (p78) along Wukang Rd.

 Dinner will be a tough call. Classy Sìchuān fare at **Pǐnchuān** (p83) or Xīnjiāng cuisine at stylish **Xībó** (p83). Or for a romantic evening, **ElEfante** (p82) ticks all the right boxes, with fine Mediterranean cuisine to boot. This is night-owl territory, so bars are everywhere.

For a local's day in the French Concession West, see p78.

Local Life

Concession-Era Architecture (p78)

♥ Best of Shànghǎi

Eating
Jian Guo 328 (p83)
Jesse (p83)
Fu 1039 (p84)
Spicy Joint (p83)
Noodle Bull (p84)

Drinking
el Cóctel (p84)
Apartment (p84)
Cotton's (p85)
Shelter (p85)
Shànghǎi Brewery (p86)

Getting There

Ⓜ **Metro** The western half of the French Concession is served by lines 1, 7 and 10. Line 10 follows Huaihai Rd east–west. Line 1 also follows Huaihai Rd east–west before veering southwest to follow Hengshan Rd. Line 7 connects the French Concession with Jìng'ān to the north, meeting up with line 1 at Changshu Rd station.

Local Life
Concession-Era Architecture

The western part of the French Concession was once one of the most desirable addresses in Shànghǎi, evident from the large and extravagant mansions scattered throughout the area. Although some of these residences are still inhabited, others have been transformed into stylish restaurants, shops, galleries and historic sites, particularly along the century-old Rte Ferguson (today's Wukang Rd).

① Yongfoo Elite

Although this 1930s **residence** (雍福会; Yǒngfú Huì; www.yongfooelite.com; 200 Yongfu Rd; 永福路200号; ⏱11.30am-midnight) was once members-only, it's since opened to the general public – great news, because the decor is absolutely stunning. Take time out for afternoon tea or return later for dinner and drinks to fully appreciate the antique-strewn setting, which includes a gorgeous carved archway from Zhèjiāng in the garden.

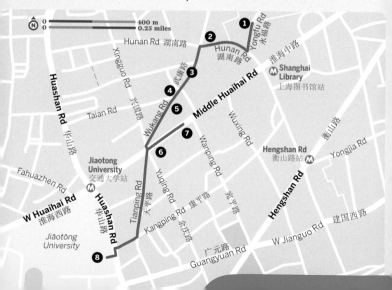

2 Ba Jin's Former Residence

This charming little pebble-dash **residence** (巴金故居; Bājīn Gùjū; 113 Wukang Rd; 武康路113号; admission free; ⏰10am-4pm Tue-Sat; Ⓜ Shanghai Library) with a delightful garden wouldn't look out of place in a leafy London suburb. It was the house of acclaimed writer Ba Jin (1904–2005), author of *Family,* from 1955 to the mid-1990s. It contains a small collection of old photos, books and manuscripts. Your passport may be needed for entry.

3 Route Ferguson

Lined with extravagant villas, Wukang Rd (originally Rte Ferguson) has been a coveted address among Shànghǎi's movers and shakers ever since its inception in 1907. More than 20 notable heritage buildings remain.

4 Leo Gallery

Drop into the red-brick Ferguson Lane complex – a haven for sun-starved diners in nice weather – for a quick tour through the **Leo Gallery** (狮语画廊; Shīyǔ Huàláng; www.leogallery.com.cn; 376 Wukang Rd; 武康路376号; admission free; ⏰11am-7pm Tue-Sun; Ⓜ Shanghai Library, Jiaotong University), which has a rotating line-up of contemporary Chinese art exhibitions.

5 Wukang Road Tourist Information Centre

This useful **centre** (武康路旅游咨询中心; Wǔkāng Lù Lǚyóu Zīxún Zhōngxīn; 393 Wukang Rd; 武康路393号; ⏰9am-5pm; Ⓜ Shanghai Library) displays scale-model concession buildings, photos of historic Shànghǎi architecture and maps of heritage buildings along Wukang Rd. It's housed in the former residence of Huang Xing (1874–1916), a revolutionary who, together with Sun Yatsen, co-founded the Republic of China.

6 Song Qingling's Former Residence

Built in the 1920s by a Greek shipping magnate, this **building** (宋庆龄故居; Sòng Qìnglíng Gùjū; 1843 Middle Huaihai Rd; 淮海中路1843号; admission ¥20; ⏰9am-4.30pm; Ⓜ Jiaotong University) became home to the wife of Sun Yatsen from 1948 to 1963 and still contains some of her original possessions. It stands across from the landmark Normandie Apartments (1924), whose covered arcade wraps around the intersection of Wukang and Huaihai Rds.

7 Shànghǎi Guqin Cultural Foundation

This **cultural centre** (上海古琴文化会; Shànghǎi Gǔqín Wénhuà Huì; ☎021 6437 4111; www.yhgy-guqin.com; 1801 Middle Huaihai Rd; 淮海中路1801号; ⏰9am-5pm; Ⓜ Shanghai Library) offers classes in a handful of traditional arts: Chinese ink painting, *wéiqí* (围棋; traditional game of Go) and the *gǔqín* (古琴; seven-string zither). Drop by to visit the peaceful 1930s villa and garden, and the students might give you a brief demonstration.

8 Jiāotōng University

Founded in 1896, Jiāotōng University has an attractive campus, especially the lawn a short walk beyond the main gate and the old **library building** (图书馆; *túshūguǎn*) opposite.

For reviews see

👁	Sights	p81
🍴	Eating	p82
🍷	Drinking	p84
★	Entertainment	p87
🛍	Shopping	p87

W Beijing Rd 北京西路

Wanhangdu Rd 万航渡路

W Nanjing Rd 南京西路

Shànghǎi Exhibition Centre

N Shaanxi Rd 陕西北路

Tourist Information & Service Centre

Jing'an Temple 静安寺站

Jing'ān Park

Middle Yan'an Rd 延安中路

Zhenning Rd 镇宁路

Yuyuan Rd 愚园路

S Shaanxi Rd 陕西南路

Julu Rd 巨鹿路

23

Fumin Rd 富民路

10

15

Dong Zhu'anbang Rd 东诸安浜路

W Yan'an Rd 延安西路

华山路

24

S Xiangyang Rd 襄阳北路

Chinese Printed Blue Nankeen Exhibition Hall

8

11

22

Xinle Rd

Hóngqiáo 🚄 (8.5km); Hóngqiáo 🚉 (9km)

Huashan Rd

Changle Rd 长乐路

Changshu Rd 常熟路

Huating Rd 华亭路

3

Donghu Rd

4

9

Propaganda Poster Art Centre

Caojiayan Rd 曹家堰路

Anfu Rd

安福路

S Wulumuqi Rd 乌鲁木齐中路

Middle Huaihai Rd 淮海中路

1

19

Jiangsu Rd 江苏路

Huashan Rd 华山路

Dìngxiāng Garden

Wuyuan Rd 五原路

20

14

12

18

Changshu Rd 常熟路站

Baoqing Rd 宝庆路

17

Middle Fuxing Rd 复兴中路

W Fuxing Rd 复兴西路

25

S Xiangyang Rd 襄阳南路

Gaoyou Rd

Yongfu Rd 永福路

Middle Huaihai Rd 淮海中路

Taojiang Rd

Shànghǎi Arts & Crafts Museum

2

Xingguo Rd 兴国路

Wukang Rd

5

16

Dongping Rd

Yueyang Rd 岳阳路

Taiyuan Rd 太原路

21

7

Taian Rd

Shanghai Library 上海图书馆站

S Wulumuqi Rd 乌鲁木齐南路

Yongjia Rd 永嘉路

Jiaotong University 交通大学站

Yaping Rd

6

Hengshan Rd 衡山路站

Wuxing Rd

Anting Rd 安亭路

W Jianguo Rd 建国西路

Jiāotōng University

Xinjing Rd 天平路

Tianping Rd

Kangping Rd 康平路

Wanping Rd

Hengshan Rd 衡山路

13

Shànghǎi South 🚉 (5km)

Zhaojiabang Rd 肇嘉浜路

0 ————— 500 m
0 ————— 0.25 miles

N

Propaganda Poster Art Centre

Sights

Propaganda Poster Art Centre

GALLERY

1 ⊙ Map p80, B3

If phalanxes of red tractors, bumper harvests, muscled peasants and lantern-jawed proletariat fire you up, this small gallery in the bowels of a residential block should intoxicate. The collection of 3000 original posters from the 1950s, '60s and '70s – the golden age of Maoist poster production – will have you weak-kneed at the cartoon world of anti-US defiance. (宣传画年画艺术中心; Xuānchuánhuà Niánhuà Yìshù Zhōngxīn; ☑021 6211 1845; Room B-OC, President Mansion, 868 Huashan Rd; 华山路868号B-OC室; admission ¥20; ⏰10am-5pm; Ⓜ Shanghai Library)

Shànghǎi Arts & Crafts Museum

MUSEUM

2 ⊙ Map p80, D3

Repositioned as a museum, this arts and crafts institute displays traditional crafts such as embroidery, paper cutting, lacquer work, jade cutting and lantern making. Watch traditional crafts being performed live by crafts-people and admire the wonderfully wrought exhibits, from jade to ivory to ink stones and beyond. The 1905 building itself is a highlight, once serving as the residence for Chen Yi, Shànghǎi's first mayor after the founding of the Chinese Communist Party (CCP). (上海工艺美术博物馆; Shànghǎi Gōngyì Měishù Bówùguǎn; 79 Fenyang Rd; 汾阳路79路; admission ¥8; ⏰9am-4pm; Ⓜ Changshu Rd)

Chinese Printed Blue Nankeen Exhibition Hall

MUSEUM

3 ⊚ Map p80, C3

Follow the blue signs through a maze of courtyards until you see bolts of blue cloth drying in the yard. Originally produced in Jiāngsū, Zhèjiāng and Guìzhōu provinces, this blue-and-white cotton fabric (sometimes called blue calico) is similar to batik, and is coloured using a starch-resist method and indigo dye bath. (中国蓝印花布馆; Zhōngguó Lán Yìnhuābù Guǎn; ☑021 5403 7947; No 24, Lane 637, Changle Rd; 长乐路 637弄24号; ◷9am-5pm; MChangshu Rd)

Eating

ElEfante

MEDITERRANEAN $$

4 ⊗ Map p80, D2

Willy Trullas Moreno's latest Shànghǎi creation sits squarely at the heart of the French Concession – in the same spot as his first venture – with a choice patio and romantic 1920s villa setting. Its tantalising Mediterranean menu with tapas-style dishes has pronounced Spanish and Italian inflections, and has local gastronomes buzzing. (☑021 5404 8085; www.el-efante.com; 20 Donghu Rd; 东湖路20号; ◷11am-3pm & 6-10.30pm Tue-Sun; MSouth Shaanxi Rd)

RICHARD I'ANSON / GETTY IMAGES ©

Chinese Printed Blue Nankeen Exhibition Hall

Pǐnchuān
SICHUANESE $$

5 Map p80, C4

Fire fiends love Sìchuān cooking, where the sophistication goes far beyond merely smothering everything with hot peppers. The telltale blend of chillies and peppercorns is best summed up in two words: *là* (辣; spicy) and *má* (麻; numbing). Even though Pǐnchuān has hit the upscale button repeatedly in the past few years, this is still a fine place to experience the tongue tingling. Try the sliced beef in spicy sauce, baked spare ribs with peanuts or *làzǐ jī* (辣子鸡; spicy chicken). The duck with sticky rice will help mitigate the damage to your tastebuds. Reserve. (品川; ☏400 820 7706; 47 Taojiang Rd; 桃江路47号; dishes ¥39-89; ⏰11am-2pm & 5-11pm; ☻; Ⓜ Changshu Rd)

Jesse
SHANGHAINESE $$

6 Map p80, A5

Jesse specialises in packing lots of people into tight spaces, so if you tend to gesture wildly when you talk, watch out with those chopsticks. This is Shanghainese home cooking at its best: crab dumplings, Grandma's braised pork and plenty of fish, drunken shrimp and eel. (吉士酒楼; Jíshì Jiǔlóu; ☏021 6282 9260; 41 Tianping Rd; 天平路41号; dishes ¥38-98; ⏰11am-4pm & 5.30pm-midnight; ☐; Ⓜ Jiaotong University)

Jian Guo 328
SHANGHAINESE $

7 Map p80, D4

Frequently crammed, this boisterous two-floor MSG-free spot tucked away on Jianguo Rd does a roaring trade on the back of fine Shànghǎi cuisine. You can't go wrong with the menu, but for pointers the deep-fried spare ribs feature succulent pork in a crispy coating, while the eggplant in casserole is a rich, thick and thumb-raising choice, high on flavour. (328 West Jianguo Rd; 建国西路328号; mains from ¥12; ⏰11am-9.30pm; ☐; Ⓜ Jiashan Rd)

Xībó
CENTRAL ASIAN $$

8 Map p80, C2

Trust Shànghǎi to serve up a stylish Xīnjiāng joint, because this isn't the type of place you're likely to find out in China's wild northwest. But who's complaining? When you need a mutton fix, beef skewers or some spicy 'big plate chicken', Xībó will do you right (and the restaurant donates healthily to charities in West China). (锡伯新疆餐厅; Xībó Xīnjiāng Cāntīng; ☏021 5403 8330; www.xiboxinjiang.com; 3rd fl, 83 Changshu Rd; 常熟路83号3楼; mains ¥35-92; ⏰noon-2.30pm & 6pm-midnight; ☐; Ⓜ Changshu Rd)

Spicy Joint
SICHUANESE $

9 Map p80, D3

If you have to have Sìchuān food, head to this place, where the blistering heat is matched only by its scorching popularity. Inexpensive (for Shànghǎi) dishes include favourites such as spicy catfish in hot chilli oil, an addictive garlic-cucumber salad, smoked-tea duck and chilli-coated lamb chops. You'll need a mobile number to secure a place in the queue. (辛香汇; Xīnxiānghui; ☑021 6470 2777; 3rd fl, K Wah Center, 1028 Middle Huaihai Rd; 淮海中路1028号嘉华中心3楼; dishes ¥12-60; ☺11am-10pm; 🛜🈸; Ⓜ South Shaanxi Rd)

Fu 1039 SHANGHAINESE $$$

10 Map p80, A2

In a three-storey 1913 villa, Fu attains an old-fashioned charm. Foodies who appreciate sophisticated surroundings and Shanghainese food on par with the decor, take note – Fu is a must. The succulent standards won't disappoint: the smoked-fish starter and stewed pork in soy sauce are recommended, with the sautéed chicken and mango and the sweet-and-sour Mandarin fish a close second. (福一零三九; Fú Yào Líng Sān Jiǔ; ☑021 5237 1878; 1039 Yuyuan Rd; 愚园路1039号; dishes ¥60-108; 🈸; Ⓜ Jiangsu Rd)

Noodle Bull NOODLES $

11 Map p80, D2

Noodle Bull is the bee's knees: far cooler than your average street-corner noodle stand (minimalist concrete chic and funky bowls), inexpensive, and boy is that broth slurpable. It doesn't matter whether you go vegetarian or for the

roasted beef noodles (¥38); it's a winner both ways. Vegetarians should zero in on the carrot-and-cucumber-sprinkled sesame-paste noodles (¥32), which are divine. (狠牛面; Hěnniú Miàn; ☑021 6170 1299; unit 3b, 291 Fumin Rd; 富民路291号3b室; noodles ¥28-35; ☺11am-midnight; 🛜🈸; Ⓜ Changshu Rd, South Shaanxi Rd)

Drinking

El Cóctel BAR

12 Map p80, B3

What do you get when you cross an ever-inventive Spanish chef with a perfectionist bartender from Japan? El Cóctel, of course – an artsy, retro cocktail lounge that mixes up damn fine drinks. The mixology list goes beyond the usual suspects: sample old-school temptations such as the black Manhattan or the Bermuda mule, but come with cash to spare. (☑021 6433 6511; 2nd fl, 47 Yongfu Rd; 永福路47号; ☺5pm-3am; Ⓜ Shanghai Library)

Apartment BAR

This trendy loft-style bar, located one floor above El Cóctel (see 12 Map p80, B3), is designed to pull in the full spectrum of 30-something professionals, with a comfort-food menu; a dance space and lounge zone; a retro bar room; and, topping it all, a terrace for views and summer BBQ action. (☑021 6437 9478; www.theapartment-shanghai.com; 3rd fl, 47 Yongfu Rd; 永福路47号; ☺5pm-late; 🛜; Ⓜ Shanghai Library)

Cotton Club (p87)

Cotton's
BAR

13 Map p80, C5

This excellent bar is perhaps the most pleasant spot in the Concession to raise a glass. Ensconced in a converted 1930s villa, the bar's interior has cosy sofas and fireplaces to snuggle around in the winter and a tiny outdoor terrace on the 2nd floor. The real draw, though, is the garden, which is intimate yet still big enough not to feel cramped. (棉花酒吧; Miánhuā Jiǔbā; 🖉021 6433 7995; www. cottons-shanghai.com; 132 Anting Rd; 安亭路132号; ⏱11am-2am Sun-Thu, to 4am Fri & Sat; 🛜; ⓂHengshan Rd, Zhaojiabang Rd)

Shelter
CLUB

14 Map p80, B3

The darling of the underground crowd, Shelter is a reconverted bomb shelter where you can count on great music, cheap drinks and a nonexistent dress code. It brings in a fantastic line-up of international DJs and hip-hop artists; the large, barely lit dance area is the place to be. Cover for big shows is usually around ¥30. (5 Yongfu Rd; 永福路5号; ⏱9pm-4am Wed-Sat; ⓂShanghai Library)

Q Local Life

Gay Times Shànghǎi

Shànghǎi's gay scene is low profile: the Chinese are a naturally undemonstrative people, their culture is conservative and the communists put gay pride low on their wish list. Yet, as a rapidly liberalising city, Shànghǎi is a natural destination for China's gays and lesbians and the annual **Shànghǎi Pride** (www.shpride.com) has been running since 2009. Our pick of gay bars includes **Shànghǎi Studio** (Map p80, A4; 嘉浓休闲; Jiānóng Xiūxián; www.shanghai-studio.com; No 4, Lane 1950, Middle Huaihai Rd; 淮海中路1950弄4号; ⏰9pm-2am; Ⓜ Jiaotong University), which transformed the cool depths of a former bomb shelter into a laid-back bar, art gallery and men's underwear shop (MANifesto; ⏰2pm to 2am), Shànghǎi's longest-running gay bar – **Eddy's Bar** (Map p80, A5; 嘉浓休; Jiānóng Xiūxián; 1877 Middle Huaihai Rd; 淮海中路1877号, 近天平路; ⏰8pm-2am; Ⓜ Jiaotong University) – a friendly place with a flash square bar to sit around, as well as a few corners to hide away in, and **390 Bar** (www.390shanghai.com; 390 Panyu Rd; 番禺路390号; ⏰6pm-late; 📶; Ⓜ Jiaotong University), one of the only LGBT clubs in town, with live music, DJs and great cocktails.

Fennel Lounge

BAR

15 🍷 Map p80, A2

Fennel is a classy cocktail lounge divided into a dining room, a cosy living-type room with a tiny stage, and a lounge area featuring a sunken bar and casual seating. An impressive drinks list, skilled bar staff and an eclectic line-up of live acoustic performances (everything from jazz to traditional Chinese music) make it a favourite with hip, cashed-up 30-somethings. (回香; Huí Xiāng; 📞021 3353 1773; 217 Zhenning Rd, entrance on Dongzhu'anbang Rd; 镇宁路217号; ⏰6pm-2am; 📶; Ⓜ Jiangsu Rd)

Shànghǎi Brewery

BREWERY

16 🍷 Map p80, C4

Hand-crafted microbrews, a big range of comfort food, pool tables and sport on TV...this massive two-storey hang-out might just have it all. Well, it certainly has enough to stand out on a strip already bursting with established names. Try the Czech-style People's Pilsner or the Hong Mei Amber Hefeweizen – a mere ¥20 during happy hour (from 2pm to 8pm). (www.shanghaibrewery.com; 15 Dongping Rd; 东平路15号; ⏰10am-2am Sun-Thu, to 3am Fri & Sat; 📶; Ⓜ Changshu Rd, Hengshan Rd)

Entertainment

Cotton Club LIVE MUSIC

17 Map p80, C3

Harlem it ain't, but this is still the best and longest-running bar for live jazz in Shànghǎi. Wynton Marsalis once stopped by to jam, forever sealing the Cotton Club's reputation as the top live-music haunt in town. It features blues and jazz groups throughout the week and the music gets going around 9pm. (棉花俱乐部; Miánhuā Jùlèbù; ☎021 6437 7110; www.thecottonclub.cn; 8 West Fuxing Rd; 复兴西路8号; ☺7.30pm-2am Tue-Sun; Ⓜ Changshu Rd)

JZ Club LIVE MUSIC

18 Map p80, B3

JZ is one of the best places in town for serious music lovers. The schedule rotates local and international groups, with sounds ranging from fusion, Latin and R&B to Chinese folk-jazz; music generally gets going around 9pm. There's a ¥50 cover on Monday, Friday and Saturday nights. It also organises the annual JZ Shànghǎi Jazz Festival. (☎021 6385 0269; www.jzclub.cn; 46 West Fuxing Rd; 复兴西路46号; ☺9pm-2am; Ⓜ Changshu Rd)

Shopping

Pīlìngpālāng – Anfu Lu CERAMICS

19 🔒 Map p80, B3

Gorgeously coloured and trendy ceramics, cloisonné and lacquer, in pieces that celebrate traditional Chinese forms while adding a funky modern and deco-inspired slant. (噼呤啪啷; www.pilingpalang.com; 183 Anfu Rd; 安福路183号; Ⓜ Changshu Rd)

Shànghǎi Arts & Crafts Museum (p81)

Lolo Love Vintage

VINTAGE

20 Map p80, B3

There's rock and roll on the stereo and a huge white rabbit, stuffed peacock and plastic cactus outside at this whacky shrine to vintage 1940s and '50s glad rags, behind the blue steel door on Yongfu Rd. It's stuffed with frocks, blouses, tops, shoes, brooches and sundry togs spilling from hangers, shelves and battered suitcases. (2 Yongfu Rd; 永福路2号; ⏰noon-10pm; Ⓜ️Shanghai Library, Changshu Rd)

Understand
Seduction & the City

Shànghǎi owes its reputation as the most fashionable city in China to the calendar poster, whose print runs once numbered in the tens of millions and whose distribution reached from China's interior to Southeast Asia. The basic idea behind the poster was to associate a product with an attractive woman, to encourage subconscious desire and consumption. Not only did calendar posters introduce new products to Chinese everywhere but also their portrayal of Shànghǎi women – wearing make-up and stylish clothing, smoking cigarettes and surrounded by foreign goods – set the standard for modern fashion that many Chinese women would dream of for decades.

OOAK Concept Boutique

JEWELLERY

21 Map p80, D4

Tall and skinny OOAK ('One of a Kind') has three floors of inspiring jewellery; catchy and attractive modern clothing for women; and bags and shoes from a host of talented big-name and aspiring independent designers from Europe and far-flung parts of the globe. (OOAK设计师品牌概念店; OOAK Shèjìshī Pǐnpái Gàiniàndiàn; www.theoook.com; 124 Taiyuan Rd; 太原路124号; ⏰11am-9pm; Ⓜ️Jiashan Rd, Hengshan Rd)

NuoMi

CLOTHING

22 Map p80, D2

This Shànghǎi-based label seems to do everything right: gorgeous dresses made from organic cotton, silk and bamboo; eye-catching jewellery fashioned from recycled materials; a sustainable business plan that gives back to the community; and even an irresistible line of kids' clothes. (糯米; Nùomǐ; www.nuomishanghai.com; 196 Xinle Rd; 新乐路196号; ⏰11am-10pm; Ⓜ️Changshu Rd)

Brocade Country

HANDICRAFTS

23 Map p80, D2

Peruse an exquisite collection of minority handicrafts from China's southwest, most of which are second-hand (ie not made for the tourist trade) and personally selected by the owner, Liu Xiaolan, a Guìzhōu native. Items for sale include embroidered wall hangings (some of which were

Madame Mao's Dowry

originally baby carriers), sashes, shoes and hats, as well as silver jewellery. (锦绣纺; Jǐnxiù Fǎng; 616 Julu Rd; 巨鹿路616号; ⏰10am-7.30pm; Ⓜ South Shaanxi Rd)

Madame Mao's Dowry
CLOTHING, SOUVENIRS

24 🔒 Map p80, D2

What better way to brighten up your hall than with a bust of Chairman Mao? Or a poster of jubilant socialist workers? Beyond the Cultural Revolution paintings and prints, there's a collection of locally designed clothing and jewellery and some fantastic cards. (毛太设计; Máotài Shèjì; ☎ 021 5403 3551; madamemaosdowry.com; 207 Fumin Rd; 富民路207号; ⏰10am-7pm; Ⓜ Jing'an Temple)

Urban Tribe
CLOTHING

25 🔒 Map p80, B3

Urban Tribe draws inspiration from the ethnic groups of China and Southeast Asia. The collection includes loose-fitting blouses, pants and jackets made of natural fabrics, and is a refreshing departure from the city's on-the-go attitude and usual taste for flamboyance. Don't miss the collection of silver jewellery, or the lovely tea garden behind the store. (城市山民; Chéngshì Shānmín; 133 West Fuxing Rd; 复兴西路133号; Ⓜ Shanghai Library)

Explore

Jìng'ān

The vibrant commercial district of Jìng'ān has evolved into a popular business, shopping and residential zone, defined by the pulsing throb of West Nanjing Rd (named Bubbling Well Rd in concession times). Art lovers can forage north to M50, Buddhists will make a beeline for the Jade Buddha Temple, while foodies will have their hands full deciding where to eat.

The Sights in a Day

☀ Jìng'ān is a fascinating neighbourhood, and there's no better way to explore it than on foot. Learn about the **local architecture** (p96) around West Nanjing Rd, where you can visit alleyway housing and one of Mao Zedong's former residences. Stop for an early lunch at **Vegetarian Lifestyle** (p101) or **Wujiang Road Food Street** (p102) and then head to **Jade Buddha Temple** (p92), or visit the temple first followed by lunch at the adjacent vegetarian canteen.

☀ Taxi over to nearby **M50** (p94), where you can sift through the experiments taking place in contemporary art and get a feel for the issues that preoccupy modern Chinese society. After a drink and a bite at **Bandu Cabin** (p102), take a taxi to **Jìng'ān Temple** (pictured left; p100), where the statuary contrasts markedly with that of Jade Buddha Temple.

☾ For dinner, go sophisticated: classy Hunanese at **Gǔyì Húnán Restaurant** (p102) or scrumptious Shànghǎi-Cantonese hybrid **Lynn** (p101), followed by an acrobatic evening at **Shànghǎi Centre Theatre** (p102).

For a local's day in Jìng'ān, see p96.

👁 Top Sights

Jade Buddha Temple (p92)

M50 (p94)

🔍 Local Life

Jìng'ān Architecture (p96)

♥ Best of Shànghǎi

Eating

Commune Social (p100)

Gǔyì Húnán Restaurant (p102)

Sumerian (p100)

Ceramics

Spin (p103)

Jǐngdézhèn Porcelain Artware (p97)

Entertainment

Shànghǎi Centre Theatre (p102)

Bandu Cabin (p102)

Getting There

Ⓜ **Metro** Line 2 runs beneath West Nanjing Rd, stopping at People's Square, West Nanjing Rd and Jìng'ān Temple. Line 7 runs from north Jìng'ān to the French Concession, with handy junctions at Jìng'ān Temple and Changshou Rd. When completed, line 13 will link Changshou Rd in north Jìng'ān with West Nanjing Rd.

Top Sights
Jade Buddha Temple

One of Shànghǎi's few active Buddhist monasteries, this temple was built between 1918 and 1928. The highlight is a transcendent Buddha made of pure jade, one of five shipped back to China by the monk Hui Gen at the turn of the 20th century, following a pilgrimage from the Buddhist island of Pǔtuóshān to Myanmar (Burma) via Tibet.

Map p98, D2

玉佛寺; Yùfó Sì

cnr Anyuan & Jiangning Rds; 安远路和江宁路街口

high/low season ¥20/10

8am-4.30pm

19 from Broadway Mansions along Tiantong Rd, M Changshou Rd

Great Treasure Hall, Jade Buddha Temple

Don't Miss

Hall of Heavenly Kings

Although you no longer enter through the original entrance hall, this hall – on your right as you come in – should be the first one you visit, with its namesake kings (Growth, Knowledge, the All-Seeing, and Protector of the Country) and a splendid statue of the Laughing Buddha back-to-back with a fabulous effigy of Weituo, the guardian of Buddhism.

Great Treasure Hall

Festooned with red lanterns and paved with slabs etched with lotus flowers, the first courtyard leads to the twin-eaved Great Treasure Hall, where worshippers pray to the past, present and future Buddhas, which are seated on splendidly carved thrones. There are also beautifully carved *luóhàn* (arhats), lashed to the walls with wires and a copper-coloured statue of Guanyin at the rear.

Jade Buddha Hall

Follow the right-hand corridor past the Hall of Heavenly Kings and the Guanyin Hall to arrive at the **Jade Buddha Hall** (admission ¥10). The absolute centrepiece of the temple is the 1.9m-high pale-green jade Buddha, which is seated upstairs. Visitors are not able to approach the statue but can admire it from a distance. Photographs are not permitted.

Ancestral Hall & Jìngyì Pool

On your right as you exit the Jade Buddha Hall is the Ancestral Hall, where Buddhist services are held. At the rear of the temple is the peaceful Jìngyì Pool (净意潭; Jìngyì Tán), which swarms with koi and multicoloured floating artificial lotus blooms, its floor glittering with coins.

☑ **Top Tips**

► In February, during the Lunar New Year, the temple is very busy, as some 20,000 Chinese Buddhists throng here to pray for prosperity.

► The surrounding shops and hawkers sell everything you need to generate good fortune, including bundles of spirit money and incense sticks.

► Look for statues of Guanyin, the goddess of mercy, throughout the temple (see understand box, p57). One is located at the rear of the Great Treasure Hall; she also has her own hall on the far side of the first courtyard.

✗ **Take a Break**

Pull up a seat alongside the monks, nuns and lay worshippers at the two-storey Buddhist **vegetarian restaurant** (玉佛寺素斋; Yùfó Sì Sùzhāi; 999 Jiangning Rd; 江宁路999号; dishes ¥18-36; ✔; Ⓜ Changshou Rd) for a meat-free feast.

Top Sights
M50

Chinese contemporary art has been the hottest thing in the art world for over a decade now, and there's no sign of the boom ending, with collectors around the world paying record prices for the work of top artists. Běijīng may dominate the art scene, but Shànghǎi has its own thriving gallery subculture, centred on this complex of industrial buildings (once a textile mill) down dusty Moganshan Rd in the north of town.

◉ Map p98, E1

M50创意产业集聚区; M50 Chuàngyì Chǎnyè Jíjùqū

50 Moganshan Rd; 莫干山路50号

admission free

Ⓜ Shanghai Railway Station

Xu Zhen – Produced by Madeln Company, courtesy of the artist and ShanghART

Don't Miss

ShanghART

The most established gallery here, the two-decades-old **ShanghART** (Xiānggénà Huàláng; www.shanghartgallery.com; Bldgs 16 & 18, M50; M50创意产业集聚区16和18号楼; Ⓜ Shanghai Railway Station) was founded by Swiss-born Lorenz Helbling in 1996. It now has two big, dramatic spaces showing the work of some of its 40 artists, including M50 pioneers Ding Yi and Zhou Tiehai.

island6

The top-notch and provocative **island6** (www.island6.org; 2nd fl, Bldg 6, M50; M50创意产业集聚区6号楼2楼; Ⓜ Shanghai Railway Station) is a collective focusing on collaborative works created in a studio behind the gallery. Known as Liu Dao in Chinese, the studio consists of an international rotating group of artists and techies, and often experiments with media such as LED art and digital works.

m97

Located across the street from M50, **m97** (www.m97gallery.com; 2nd fl, 97 Moganshan Rd; 莫干山路97号2楼; Ⓜ Shanghai Railway Station) is the largest photography gallery in Shànghǎi, representing some two dozen China-based photographers.

Other Spaces

Huang Yunhe's **OFoto** (2nd fl, Bldg 13, M50; M50创意产业集聚区13号楼2楼; Ⓜ Shanghai Railway Station) features contemporary photography exhibitions. For paint and art materials, there's well-stocked **Espace Pébéo** (http://en.pebeo.com/Pebeo; 1st fl, Bldg 0, M50 Moganshan Rd; 莫干山M50号0号楼1楼; ⏱ 9.30am-6pm; Ⓜ Shanghai Railway Station); for photo-developing courses and prints, try **Dark Room** (☎ 021 6276 9657; Rm 107, Bldg 17, 50 Moganshan Rd; M50创意产业集聚区17号楼107室; Ⓜ Shanghai Railway Station).

☑ Top Tips

▶ Most galleries are open from 10am to 6pm; the majority close on Monday.

▶ There are a lot of commercial spaces here selling unimaginative, mass-produced artwork. It can be hard to recognise initially, so start with recommended galleries for the best introduction. As a general rule, you can skip buildings 3 and 4 near the entrance.

✘ Take a Break

A charming and individual place to grab a bowl of noodles, scarf a snack, sip a drink and rest your feet, Bandu Cabin (p102) in M50 is a relaxing choice, with weekly traditional Chinese music concerts.

Local Life
Jìng'ān Architecture

Jìng'ān boasts an unusual melange of architectural styles, ranging from Shànghǎi-style row housing and 1920s apartment blocks to Christian and Jewish temples of worship. One of the greatest concentrations of old buildings can be found on North Shaanxi Rd (formerly Seymour Rd). For a snapshot of everyday Shànghǎi life, this is a great place to start.

❶ Bubbling Well Road Apartments

One of the most delightful surviving new-style *lǐlòng* (里弄; alley) housing complexes in Shànghǎi, Bubbling Well Road Apartments (静安别墅; Jìng'ān Biéshù) consists of three-storey red-brick houses built between 1928 and 1932. It's a great spot to observe daily residential life and explore a new crop of tiny ground-floor cafes and boutiques.

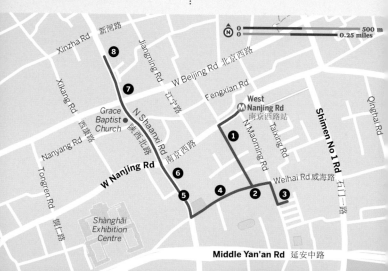

❷ Sun Court

Down the street from Bubbling Well is **Sun Court** (651 Weihai Rd; 威海路651号; Ⓜ West Nanjing Rd), a multistorey apartment building completed in 1928. Although it was named after real-estate mogul Sun Chunsheng (1899–1974), the Chinese translator mistakenly used 太阳 ('sun' in the sky) instead of 孙 (Sun's name) when assigning the Chinese name. Peek into the leafy inner courtyard.

❸ Mao Zedong's Former Residence

Mao lived **here** (毛泽东旧居; Máo Zédōng Jiùjū; No 5-9, 120 North Maoming Rd; 茂名北路120弄5-9号; admission free; ⊘9-11.30am & 1-4.30pm; Ⓜ Jing'an Temple) in the latter half of 1924 with his second wife, Yang Kaihui, and their two children. The residence is a beautiful example of *shíkùmén* (石库门; stone-gate house) architecture. You'll need your passport to enter.

❹ Tea Shop

The **Xiao Ye Tea Shop** (小叶名茶; Xiǎoyè Míng Chá; 686 Weihai Rd; ⊘7.30am-9.30pm) at 686 Weihai Rd has a good collection of *pu'erh* (aged fermented tea from Yunnan) cakes and bricks lining the walls, as well as loose-leaf oolong, white and herbal teas for sale. The back room also sells teapots and utensils.

❺ North Shaanxi Road

The garden residence (1918) at No 186 once belonged to Wúxī native Rong Zongjing, one of Shànghǎi's most powerful industrialists at the time. Rong Zongjing's nephew, Rong Yiren, was one of the rare individuals with a capitalist background to succeed in communist China, becoming vice mayor of Shànghǎi in 1957 and later vice president of the country from 1993 to 1998.

❻ Jǐngdézhèn Porcelain Artware

This is one of the best **stores** (景德镇艺术瓷器; Jǐngdézhèn Yìshù Cíqì; ☎021 6253 8865; 212 North Shaanxi Rd; 陕西北路212号; ⊘10am-9pm; Ⓜ West Nanjing Rd) for high-quality traditional Chinese porcelain. Blue-and-white vases, plates, teapots and cups are among the many choices. International shipping available.

❼ Sea-Salt Coffee Break

Near Grace Baptist Church at No 375 (it moved here in 1942) is Taiwanese coffee-and-tea chain **Café 85°C** (85度C咖啡店; Bāwǔ Dù C Kāfēidiàn; 408 North Shaanxi Rd; 陕西北路408号; ⊘24hr; Ⓜ West Nanjing Rd). Drop in for quality, inexpensive coffee (including sea-salt coffee) and tea, and pick up a few of those unusual pastries while you're at it.

❽ Ohel Rachel Synagogue

This **synagogue** (拉结会堂; Lājié Huìtáng; 500 North Shaanxi Rd; 陕西北路500号; Ⓜ West Nanjing Rd) was built by Jacob Sassoon in 1920, and was the first of seven synagogues built in Shànghǎi (only two remain). It was constructed in the Greek Revival style, inspired by the Sephardic synagogues of London. Unfortunately, it's closed to the public.

A **B** **C** **D**

1

N Zhongshan Rd
中山北路

Ⓜ Zhenping Rd
镇坪路站

Yichang Rd
宜昌路

N Shaanxi Rd 陕西北路

Aomen Rd 澳门路

Aomen Rd 澳门路

Putuo Rd

Xikang Rd 西康路

Chángshòu Park
Park

Changshou Rd 长寿路

Jiangning Rd 江宁路

Changhua Rd

Changde Rd 常德路

Ⓞ Jade Buddha Temple

Suzhou Creek (Wúsōng River)

2

W. Guangfu Rd

Ⓜ Changshou Rd
长寿路站

Xinhui Rd

Anyuan Rd 安远路

N Shaanxi Rd

3

Changning Rd 长宁路

S Wuning Rd 武宁南路

Yuyao Rd 余姚路

Changping Rd
昌平路

Yanping Rd

Jiaozhou Rd

Changde Rd 常德路

8 Ⓔ

Ⓜ Changping Rd
昌平路站

Xikang Rd 西康路

Kangding Rd 康定路

Xinzha Rd 新闸路

4

Kangding Rd 康定路

Wuding Rd 武定路

Jiaozhou Rd 胶州路

Wanhangdu Rd 万航渡路

5

Wanhangdu Rd
万航渡路

Jìng'ān Temple
静安寺

Ⓧ 7

1 Ⓜ Jing'an Temple
静安寺站

Jìng'ān Park

Yuyuan Rd 愚园路

For reviews see		
Ⓞ Top Sights	p92
Ⓞ Sights	p100
Ⓧ Eating	p100
Ⓠ Drinking	p102
Ⓢ Entertainment	p102
Ⓢ Shopping	p103

⊙ *M50*

E   F   G   H

Ⓜ Shànghǎi Railway Station 上海火车站

◉ⓝ 0 _____ 500 m
0 _____ 0.25 miles

Moganshan Rd 莫干山路

W Tianmu Rd 天目西路

Middle Tianmu Rd

Haining Rd 海宁路

Meiyuan Rd

Minli Rd

汉中路

Hanzhong Rd

Hengtong Rd

Datong Rd 大统路

Wuzhen Rd 乌镇路

Jinyuan Rd 晋元路

Chang'an Rd 长安路

Yutong Rd

Hengfeng Rd 恒丰路

Suzhou Creek (Wùsōng River)

Ⓜ Hanzhong Rd 汉中路站

Guangfu Rd 光复路

S Suzhou Rd 南苏州路

Datian Rd 大田路

Xinzha Rd 新闸路

Ⓜ Xinzha Rd 新闸路站

Haifang Rd

Changping Rd

Moganshan Rd

Wuding Rd 武定路

Shanhaiguan Rd 山海关路

Jiangning Rd 江宁路

❹ ✕ 江宁路

Shimen No 2 Rd 石门二路

⓾

Xinzha Rd 新闸路

W Beijing Rd 北京西路

Huanghe Rd 黄河路

Fengyang Rd 凤阳路

Xinchang Rd

People's Park

❷ ✕

W Beijing Rd 北京西路

Fengxian Rd

Wujiang Rd

Shimen No 1 Rd 石门一路

Qinghai Rd 青海路

N Chengdu Rd 成都北路

W Nanjing Rd 南京西路

N Huangpi Rd 黄陂北路

Jiangyin Rd

❺

Fengxian Rd

❸

Ⓜ West Nanjing Rd 南京西路站

Westgate Mall

N Maoming Rd

Weihai Rd 威海路

Wusheng Rd 武胜路

Dagu Rd

Shànghǎi Centre

Tongren Rd 铜仁路

❻ ✕

⓽

W Nanjing Rd 南京西路

Shànghǎi Exhibition Centre

N Shaanxi Rd

Dagu Rd

Guǎngchǎng Park

Middle Yan'an Rd 延安中路

S Shaanxi Rd 陕西南路

S Maoming Rd

Rujin No 1 Rd 瑞金一路

S Chengdu Rd

Changle Rd

Sights

Jìng'ān Temple

BUDDHIST TEMPLE

1 Map p98, D5

Its roof work an incongruous, shimmering mirage amid West Nanjing Rd's soaring skyscrapers, Jìng'ān Temple is a sacred portal to the Buddhist world that partly, at least, underpins this metropolis of 24 million souls. There are fewer devotees than at the neighbourhood's popular Jade Buddha Temple, but over a decade's restoration has fashioned a workable temple at the very heart of Shànghǎi. Its spectacular position among the district's soaring skyscrapers makes for eye-catching photos, and the temple emits an air of reverence. (静安寺; Jìng'ān Sì; 1686-1688 West Nanjing Rd; 南京西路1686-1688号; admission ¥50; ⏰7.30am-5pm; Ⓜ Jing'an Temple)

Eating

Sumerian

CAFE $

2 Map p98, E4

Run by a bright and sunny Californian and a sprightly Chinese, good-looking Sumerian packs a lot into a small space, with bagels, pumpkin soup, roasted vegetable salads, wraps and standout coffees (Mexican Pluma Real Organic, Colombian Popayan decaf). (415 North Shaanxi Rd; 陕西北路415号; mains from ¥20; ⏰7.30am-7.30pm; ⚡🔋; Ⓜ West Nanjing Rd)

Baker & Spice

CAFE $

This jam-packed cafe at the Shànghǎi Centre (see 9 ⭐ Map p98, E4), has long

wooden tables and a tempting array of fresh pastries, bread, salads and sandwiches – don't miss the nutty carrot cake. (Shànghǎi Centre, 1376 West Nanjing Rd; 南京西路1376号; dishes from ¥40; ⏰7am-10pm; 📶✏; Ⓜ Jing'an Temple, West Nanjing Rd)

Wagas

CAFE $

3 Map p98, F4

Express sandwiches are half-price before 10am weekdays; there are after-6pm deals; and you can hang out here for hours with your tablet and not be shooed away – need we say more? Hip Wagas is the best and most dependable of the local cafes, with chilled beats, tantalising wraps, salads and sandwiches. (沃歌斯; Wògēsī; B11A, Citic Sq, 1168 West Nanjing Rd; 南京西路1168号中信泰富地下一层11A室; mains ¥48-60; ⏰7am-10pm; ♿📶📱; Ⓜ West Nanjing Rd)

Commune Social

TAPAS $$

4 Map p98, E3

Dividing neatly into upstairs cocktail bar with terrace, downstairs open-kitchen tapas bar and dessert bar, this natty Neri & Hu–designed Jason Atherton venture blends a stylish, yet relaxed vibe with some sensational international dishes, exquisitely presented by chef Scott Melvin. It's the talk of the town, but it has a no-reservations policy, so prepare to queue. (食社; Shíshè; www.communesocial.com; 511 Jiangning Rd; 江宁路511号; mains ¥58-398; ⏰noon-2.30pm & 6-10.30pm Tue-Fri, noon-3pm & 6-10.30pm Sat, to 3pm Sun; 📱; Ⓜ Changping Rd)

靜安寺

Jing'ān Temple

Vegetarian Lifestyle

CHINESE, VEGETARIAN $$

5 🍴 Map p98, F4

These folks are maximising meat-free goodness with organic, vegetarian fare fashioned for the masses. There are loads of clever dishes, including soup served in a pumpkin, but tops are the sweet Wúxī 'spare ribs', stuffed with lotus root of course, and claypots galore. It's MSG-free and cooks go light on the oil. (枣子树; Zǎozǐshù; ☎021 6215 7566; www.jujubetree.com; 258 Fengxian Rd; 奉贤路258号; dishes ¥25-70; ⊙11am-9.30pm; 🚇🈂; Ⓜ West Nanjing Rd)

Lynn

SHANGHAINESE $$

6 🍴 Map p98, E4

Lynn offers consistently good, cleverly presented dishes in plush but unfussy surroundings. The lunch dim-sum menu offers a range of delicate dumplings, while dinner delivers more traditional Shanghainese dishes, such as eggplant with minced pork in a garlic and chilli sauce. More adventurous standouts include the sautéed chicken with sesame pockets and deep-fried spare ribs with honey and garlic. (琳怡; Lín Yí; ☎021 6247 0101; 99-1 Xikang Rd; 西康路99-1号; dishes ¥50-125; ⊙11.30am-10.30pm; 🈂; Ⓜ West Nanjing Rd)

Local Life
Wujiang Road Food Street

This pedestrian **food street** (Map p98, F4; Wujiang Rd; 吴江路; meals from ¥30; Ⓜ West Nanjing Rd) has still got the goods when it comes to snack food. If you can beat the mealtime rush, the first spot to go scavenging is the multistorey building at No 269 (above one of the West Nanjing Rd metro exits). Down at street level, you'll find plenty of cafes, Japanese ramen chains, ice-cream vendors and stalls selling more traditional snacks, such as roasted chestnuts.

Din Tai Fung   DUMPLING $$

Located in the Shànghǎi Centre (see 9 ✪ Map p98, E4), Din Tai Fung has to-die-for dumplings and flawless service from Taiwan's most famous dumpling chain. Reserve ahead. (鼎泰丰; Dǐng Tài Fēng; 🕿 021 6289 9182; Shànghǎi Centre, 1376 West Nanjing Rd; 南京西路1376号; 10 dumplings ¥58-88; ⏰ 10am-10pm; 🚼 🅿; Ⓜ Jing'an Temple, West Nanjing Rd)

Gǔyì Húnán Restaurant   HUNANESE $$

7 Map p98, D5

Classy Hunanese dining and mouth-watering cumin ribs next to Jìng'ān Temple. (古意湘味浓; Gǔyì Xiāngwèinóng; 🕿 021 6232 8377; 8th fl, City Plaza, 1618 West Nanjing Rd; 南京西路1618号8楼久百城市广场; dishes ¥38-98; 🅿; Ⓜ Jing'an Temple)

Drinking
B&C   BAR

8 🚾 Map p98, D3

You get welcoming hugs from sociable co-owner Candy at this huge old-school bar. Prices are low – in dive territory – with pool and darts for those unable to just sit and yak bar-side, while Bon Jovi and Duran Duran transport everyone back to the good old days of big bad hairstyles. (685 Xikang Rd; 西康路685号; ⏰ 6pm-2am; Ⓜ Changping Rd)

Entertainment
Shànghǎi Centre Theatre   ACROBATICS

9 ✪ Map p98, E4

The Shànghǎi Acrobatics Troupe has popular performances here most nights at 7.30pm. It's a short but fun show and is high on the to-do list of most first-time visitors. Buy tickets a couple of days in advance from the ticket office on the right-hand side at the entrance to the Shànghǎi Centre. (上海商城剧院; Shànghǎi Shāngchéng Jùyuàn; 🕿 021 6279 8948; Shànghǎi Centre, 1376 West Nanjing Rd; 南京西路1376号; tickets ¥180, ¥240 & ¥300; Ⓜ Jing'an Temple)

Bandu Cabin   LIVE MUSIC

Located in the M50 complex (see ◎ Map p98, E1), with charmingly eclectic and mismatched furniture, this laid-back cafe–record label serves up noodles, drinks and snacks, along with traditional Chinese music concerts on Saturday at 7.30pm (¥50). Phone ahead on Friday to reserve seats. There's also a quality selection of Chinese folk-music CDs. (半度音乐; Bàndù Yīnyuè; ☏ 021 6276 8267; www.bandumusic.com; Bldg 11, 50 Moganshan Rd; 莫干山路50号11号楼; ⏰10am-6.30pm Sun-Fri, to 10pm Sat; Ⓜ Shanghai Railway Station)

Shopping

Spin CERAMICS

🔟 🔒 Map p98, E3

High on creative flair, Spin brings Chinese ceramics up to speed with its oblong teacups, twisted sake sets and all manner of cool plates, chopstick holders, and 'kung fu' and 'exploded pillar' vases. Pieces are never overbearing but trendily lean towards the whimsical, geometric, thoughtful and elegantly fashionable. (旋; Xuán; 360 Kangding Rd; 康定路360号; ⏰11am-8pm; Ⓜ Changping Rd)

Han City Fashion & Accessories Plaza CLOTHING

11️⃣ 🔒 Map p98, G4

This unassuming-looking building is a popular location to pick up knock-offs, with hundreds of stalls spread across four floors. Rummage for bags, belts, jackets, shoes, suitcases, sunglasses, ties, T-shirts and electronics. Prices can be inflated, so bargain hard. (韩城服饰礼品广场; Hánchéng Fúshì Lǐpǐn Guǎngchǎng; 580 West Nanjing Rd; 南京西路580号; ⏰10am-10pm; Ⓜ West Nanjing Rd)

Amy Lin's Pearls PEARLS

Located in the Han City Fashion & Accessories Plaza (see 11️⃣ 🔒 Map p98, G4), Amy Lin's Pearls is the most reliable retailer of pearls of all colours and sizes. Both freshwater pearls (from ¥80), including prized black Zhèjiāng pearls (from ¥3000), and saltwater pearls (from ¥200) are available here. The staff speaks English and will string your selection for you. This place sells jade and jewellery, too. (艾敏林氏珍珠; Àimǐn Línshì Zhēnzhū; room 30, 3rd fl, 580 West Nanjing Rd; 南京西路580号3楼30号; ⏰10am-8pm; Ⓜ West Nanjing Rd)

Art Deco ANTIQUES

For stylish period furnishings, stop by artist Ding Yi's gallery in the M50 complex (see ◉ Map p98, E1). His standout antique collection includes folding screens, armoires, tables and chairs, with a few vintage poster girls on the walls to help cast that 1930s spell. (凹凸家具库; Āotū Jiājù Kù; ☏ 021 6277 8927; Bldg 7, 50 Moganshan Rd; 莫干山路50号7号楼; ⏰10am-6pm Tue-Sun; Ⓜ Shanghai Railway Station)

Explore

Pǔdōng

Pǔdōng is one of those places that most visitors know by name well before setting foot in Shànghǎi. In just 25 years, the district has gone from boggy farmland to China's economic powerhouse, a place where Maglev trains glide swiftly into a universe of soaring skyscrapers and scurrying suits. Sky-high observation platforms and good museums make it worth the visit.

The Sights in a Day

 There's no better way to start a day in Pǔdōng than at the **Shànghǎi History Museum** (p108), a fun and interactive look at the city's past. Once you've soaked up all the history you can handle, it's time to break for lunch, a short walk away at **South Beauty** (p110).

A hop, skip and three stops down metro line 2 is the **Science & Technology Museum** (p110). Kids will be interested in the museum itself, but most people shuttle out here for the **AP Xīnyáng Fashion & Gifts Market** (p111), the city's largest shopping market that also includes pearls and a fabric and tailoring section.

You'll want to get back to a viewing platform before dusk arrives. Head up to the top of one of several skyscrapers in the area – top picks are the **Shànghǎi Tower** (p107), the **Shànghǎi World Financial Center** (p107) or the **Jīnmào Tower** (p108). Alternatively, stop for a drink with awesome views as standard at **Flair** (p111).

 Best of Shànghǎi

Architecture
Shànghǎi Tower (p107)

Shànghǎi World Financial Center (p107)

Jīnmào Tower (p108)

Museums & Galleries
Shànghǎi History Museum (p108)

Green Spaces
Riverside Promenade (p109)

Drinking
Flair (p111)

Getting There

Ⓜ **Metro** Line 2 powers through several stations in Pǔdōng, including Lujiazui, Century Ave and the Science & Technology Museum. Lines 2, 4, 6 and 9 converge at Century Ave. The former World Expo area is served by line 8; descend at the China Art Museum stop.

⛴ **Ferry** Runs regularly between Pǔxī and Pǔdōng for the six-minute trip (¥2).

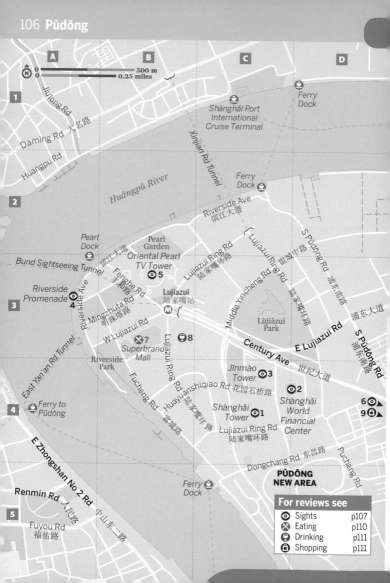

A **B** **C** **D**

N 0 500 m
0 0.25 miles

1

Jiǔ long Rd 九龙路

Daming Rd 大名路

Huangpu Rd

Huángpǔ River 黄浦江

Xúnjian Rd Tunnel

Shànghǎi Port International Cruise Terminal

Ferry Dock

2

Ferry Dock

Riverside Ave 滨江大道

3

Pearl Dock

滨江大道

Bund Sightseeing Tunnel

Pearl Garden

Oriental Pearl TV Tower ◎ **5**

Fenghe Rd 枫和路

Lujiazui Ring Rd 陆家嘴环路

Lujiazui Ring Rd 银城中路

S Pǔdōng Rd 浦东南路

Riverside Promenade ◎ **4**

Riverside Ave

Mingzhuta Rd 明珠塔路

W Lujiazui Rd

Lùjiāzuǐ 陆家嘴站 Ⓜ

Middle Yincheng Rd

Lùjiāzuǐ Park

S Pǔdōng Rd 浦东南路

浦东大道

4

East Yan'an Rd Tunnel

Riverside Park

W Lujiazui Rd

◎ **7**

Superbrand Mall

Lujiazui Ring Rd 陆家嘴环路

◎ **8**

Huayuanshiqiao Rd 花园石桥路

Fucheng Rd 富城路

Jīnmào Tower ◎ **3**

Century Ave 世纪大道

E Lujiazui Rd

Ferry to Pǔdōng

Shànghǎi Tower ◎ **1**

Lujiazui Ring Rd 陆家嘴环路

◎ **2** Shànghǎi World Financial Center

6 ◎ ▶
9 🏠 ▶

5

E Zhongshan No 2 Rd

Renmin Rd 人民路 中山东二路

Fuyou Rd 福佑路

Ferry Dock

Dongchang Rd 东昌路

Pucheng Rd

PǓDŌNG NEW AREA

For reviews see	
◎ Sights	p107
✗ Eating	p110
🍷 Drinking	p111
🏠 Shopping	p111

WANGWUKONG / GETTY IMAGES ©

Shànghǎi skyscrapers

Sights

Shànghǎi Tower BUILDING

1 ⊙ Map p106, C4

China's tallest building dramatically twists skywards from its footing in Lùjiāzuǐ. The 121-storey 632m-tall Gensler-designed Shànghǎi Tower topped out in August 2013 and was set to fully open by 2016. The spiral-shaped tower will house office space, entertainment venues, retail outlets, a conference centre, a luxury hotel and 'sky lobbies'. The gently corkscrewing form – its nine interior cylindrical units wrapped in two glass skins – is the world's second-tallest building at

the time of writing. (上海中心大厦; Shànghǎi Zhōngxīn Dàshà; www.shanghaitower. com.cn; cnr Middle Yincheng & Huayuanshiqiao Rds; Ⓜ Lujiazui)

Shànghǎi World Financial Center BUILDING

2 ⊙ Map p106, D4

Although trumped by the adjacent Shànghǎi Tower as the city's most stratospheric building, the awe-inspiring 492m-high Shànghǎi World Financial Center is an astonishing sight, even more so come nightfall when its 'bottle opener' top dances with lights. There are three observation decks here on levels 94, 97 and

ITAR-TASS PHOTO AGENCY / ALAMY STOCK PHOTO ©

Wax figures at the Shànghǎi History Museum

100, with head-spinningly altitude-adjusted ticket prices and wow-factor elevators thrown in. (上海环球金融中心; Shànghǎi Huánqiú Jīnróng Zhōngxīn; ☑021 5878 0101; http://swfc-shanghai.com; 100 Century Ave; 世纪大道100号; observation deck adult 94th fl/94th, 97th & 100th fl ¥120/180, child under 140cm ¥60/90; ☉8am-11pm, last entry 10pm; Ⓜ Lujiazui)

Jīnmào Tower

BUILDING

3 ◎ Map p106, C4

Resembling an art deco take on a pagoda, this crystalline edifice is by far the most attractive of the Shànghǎi World Financial Center (SWFC), Shànghǎi Tower, Jīnmào Tower triumvirate. It's essentially an office block with the high-altitude **Grand Hyatt** (金茂君悦大酒店; Jīnmào Jūnyuè Dàjiǔdiàn; ☑021 5049 1234; www.shanghai.grand.hyatt.com; Jinmao Tower, 88 Century Ave; 世纪大道88号金茂大厦; d from ¥2000-2450; ❄@☎❄; Ⓜ Lujiazui) renting space from the 53rd to 87th floors. Zip up in the elevators to the 88th-floor observation deck, accessed from the separate podium building to the side of the main tower (aim for dusk for both day and night views). (金茂大厦; Jīnmào Dàshà; ☑021 5047 5101; 88 Century Ave; 世纪大道88号; adult/student/child ¥120/90/60; ☉8.30am-9.30pm; Ⓜ Lujiazui)

Shànghǎi History Museum

MUSEUM

Housed in the Oriental Pearl TV Tower basement (see **5** ◎ Map p106, B3), the entire family will enjoy this informative museum with a fun presentation on old Shànghǎi. Learn how the city prospered on the back of the cotton trade and junk transportation, when it was known as 'Little Sūzhōu'. Life-sized models of traditional shops are staffed by realistic waxworks, amid a wealth of historical detail, including a boundary stone from the International Settlement and one of the bronze lions that originally guarded the entrance to the HSBC bank on the Bund. (上海城市历史发展陈列馆; Shànghǎi Chéngshì Lìshǐ Fāzhǎn Chénlièguǎn; ☑021 5879 8888; Oriental Pearl TV Tower basement; admission ¥35, English audio tour ¥30; ☉8am-9.30pm; Ⓜ Lujiazui)

Riverside Promenade WATERFRONT

4 ◎ Map p106, A3

Hands down the best stroll in Pǔdōng. The sections of promenade alongside Riverside Ave on the eastern bank of the Huángpǔ River offer splendid views to the Bund across the way. Choicely positioned cafes look out over the water. (滨江大道; Bīnjiāng Dàdào; ⊙6.30am-11pm; Ⓜ Lujiazui)

Oriental Pearl TV Tower BUILDING

5 ◎ Map p106, B3

Love it or hate it, you won't be indifferent to this 468m-tall poured-concrete tripod tower, especially at night, when it dazzles. Sucking in streams of visitors, the Deng Xiaoping–era design is inadvertently retro, but socialism with Chinese characteristics was always cheesy back then. The highlight is the excellent Shànghǎi History Museum in the basement. You can queue up for views of Shànghǎi, but there are better views elsewhere and the long lines are matched by a torturous ticketing system. (东方明珠广播电视塔; Dōngfāng Míngzhū Guǎngbō Diànshì Tǎ; ☑021 5879 1888; ⊙8am-10pm, revolving restaurant 11am-2pm & 5-9pm; Ⓜ Lujiazui)

PAUL BROWN / ALAMY STOCK PHOTO ©

Oriental Pearl TV Tower, principal designers Jiang Huan Chen, Lin Benlin, and Zhang Xiulin

Shànghǎi Science & Technology Museum

Shànghǎi Science & Technology Museum MUSEUM

6 Map p106, D4

You need to do a huge amount of walking to get about this seriously spaced-out museum, but there are some fascinating exhibits, from relentless Rubik's-cube-solving robots to mechanical archers. There's even the chance to take penalty kicks against a computerised goalkeeper. (上海科技馆; Shànghǎi Kējìguǎn; ☑021 6862 2000; www.sstm.org.cn; 2000 Century Ave; 世纪大道2000号; adult/student/child under 1.3m ¥60/45/free; ☺9am-5.15pm Tue-Sun, last tickets 4.30pm; Ⓜ Science & Technology Museum)

Eating

South Beauty SICHUANESE $

7 Ⓧ Map p106, B3

This smart restaurant with vermilion leather furniture and silky white tablecloths on the 10th floor of the Superbrand Mall cooks up classic dishes from fiery Chóngqìng, Chéngdū and the south. The scorching boiled beef with hot pepper in chilli oil (¥48) opens the sweat pores, while the piquant *mápō dòufu* (麻婆豆腐; ¥38) arrives in a scarlet oily sauce. Divine. (俏江南; Qiào Jiāngnán; ☑021 5047 1817; 10th fl, Superbrand Mall, 168 West Lujiazui Rd; 陆家嘴西路168号正大广场10楼; dishes from ¥20; ☺11am-10pm; Ⓕ; ⓂLujiazui)

Drinking

Flair BAR

8 Map p106, B3

Wow your date with Shànghǎi's most intoxicating nocturnal visuals from the 58th floor of the Ritz-Carlton, where Flair nudges you that bit closer to the baubles of the Oriental Pearl TV Tower. If it's raining, you'll end up inside, but that's OK as the chilled-out interior is supercool and there's a minimum price (¥400) for sitting outside. (58th fl, Ritz-Carlton Shanghai Pudong, 8 Century Ave; 世纪大道8号58楼; cocktails ¥90; ⏰5am-2am; 🛜; MLujiazui)

Shopping

AP Xīnyáng Fashion & Gifts Market SOUVENIRS

9 Map p106, D4

This mammoth underground market is Shànghǎi's largest collection of shopping stalls. There's tons of merchandise and fakes, from suits to moccasins, glinting copy watches, Darth Vader toys, jackets, Lionel Messi football strips, T-shirts, Indian saris, Angry Birds bags, Bob Marley Bermuda shorts, Great Wall snow globes: everything under the sun. (亚太新阳服饰礼品市场; Yàtài Xīnyáng Fúshì Lǐpǐn Shìchǎng; ⏰10am-8pm; MScience & Technology Museum)

Top Sights
Qībǎo

Getting There

Qībǎo is located in western Shànghǎi.

M Metro Take line 9 to Qibao station. It's a 20-minute ride from Xujiahui station.

Should you tire of Shànghǎi's incessant quest for modernity, tiny Qībǎo (七宝) is only a hop, skip and metro ride away. An ancient settlement that prospered during the Ming and Qing dynasties, it is dotted with traditional historic architecture, threaded by small, busy alleyways and cut by a picturesque canal. If you can blot out the crowds, Qībǎo brings you the flavours of old China, along with huge doses of entertainment.

Teahouse in the Qībǎo Old Town

Don't Miss

Cotton Textile Mill
Cotton was Qībǎo's main industry during the Ming and Qing dynasties. This recreated mill, housed in a former residence, takes you through the entire production process and has displays of old tools, photos and clothing.

Shadow Puppet Museum
This museum provides a brief history of local shadow puppetry, one of China's oldest and most enduring forms of folk art. At its most sophisticated, a travelling troupe would have consisted of five people (the puppeteer, three musicians and a singer). Try to check out the two-hour **performances** (⊙1-3pm Wed & Sun).

Old Trades House
The Old Trades House is a waxworks museum that introduces the traditional trades practised in a small Chinese town, from bamboo weaving and fortune-telling to scale making and carpentry.

Zhou's Miniature Carving Gallery
Perhaps the most unusual sight in Qībǎo is this two-storey gallery, which showcases the miniature carvings done by a father and daughter. The highlights are the extraordinarily detailed reproductions of different characters' rooms from the 18th-century classic novel *Hong Lou Meng* (Dream of Red Mansions).

Other Sights
At No 9 Nan Dajie is a traditional teahouse with **storytelling performances** (⊙12.30-2.30pm; admission incl pot of tea ¥2), the only one of its kind in Shànghǎi. Half-hour **boat rides** (per person ¥10; ⊙8.30am-5pm) slowly ferry passengers along the canal. Also worth ferreting out is the **Catholic Church** (天主教堂; 50 Nanjie; 南街50号), off Qibao Nanjie, south of the canal.

2 Minzhu Rd, Mǐnháng district; 闵行区民主路2号

high/low season ¥45/30

⊙sights 8.30am-4.30pm

Ⓜ Qibao

☑ Top Tips
▶ There are nine official sights included in the through ticket, though you can skip the ticket and just pay ¥5 to ¥10 per sight as you go.

✕ Take a Break
At the main bridge, you'll find excellent crab dumplings at **Bǎinián Lóngpáo** (百年龙袍; 15 Bei Daijie, Qībǎo; 七宝古镇北大街15号; dumplings from ¥15; ⊙6.30am-8.30pm; Ⓜ Qibao).

South of the canal, Nan Dajie is full of snacks and small eateries, such as No 26, which sells sweet *tāngyuán* (汤圆) dumplings.

The Best of
Shànghǎi

M on the Bund (p40)

Best Walks
North Bund

🏃 The Walk

The Bund is most famous for the majestic facades that line the Huángpǔ River, but don't miss the less-known northern end, which is the site of one of Shànghǎi's most ambitious redevelopment projects. Known as the Rockbund, the renovations here were funded by the Rockefeller Group and include landmark buildings, such as the former British Consulate and the YWCA Building.

Start Broadway Mansions; Ⓜ Tiantong Rd or taxi

Finish Yuanmingyuan Apartments; Ⓜ East Nanjing Rd

Length 800m; 45 minutes

🍴 Take a Break

Cafe at 1 (45 Huqiu Rd; 虎丘路45号; mains from ¥30; ⏰10am-10pm; 🔊 📶; Ⓜ East Nanjing Rd) on Huqiu Rd, just west of Yuanmingyuan Rd, is a handy and comfortable spot for a coffee and a snack, while the line-up of bars and restaurants on the Bund is just a few minutes' walk away.

The Bund (p24)

❶ Broadway Mansions

Broadway Mansions was built as an exclusive art deco apartment block in 1934, but its commanding vantage point made it a favourite of military officers – at first the Japanese, then, postwar, the US.

❷ Astor House Hotel

This landmark **edifice** was established in 1846 as the Richards Hotel and was one of Shànghǎi's most prestigious hotels during the golden years.

❸ Wàibáidù Bridge

Wàibáidù Bridge, which crosses Sūzhōu Creek to connect Hóngkǒu with the Bund, was China's first steel bridge. An earlier bridge, the Wills' Bridge (1856), levied a toll to cross. Foreigners were apparently allowed to pay on credit, but not the Chinese, and it became renowned as a symbol of foreign oppression.

❹ Former British Consulate

The original **British Consulate** was one

of the first foreign buildings to go up in Shànghǎi in 1852, though it was destroyed in a fire and replaced with the current structure in 1873. Now renovated, it is used as a financiers' club and hosts private functions. Also within the grounds are the former **Consul's Residence** (1884) – now a flagship Patek Philippe store – and several century-old magnolia trees.

❺ Union Church

Heritage buildings on South Suzhou Rd include the **Church Apartments** (1899) at No 79, and the Romanesque-style **Union Church** (1886) at No 107. Across the road is the **Former Shànghǎi Rowing Club** (1905) at No 76; with a filled-in swimming pool alongside it.

❻ China Baptist Publication Building

Yuanmingyuan Rd was once home to several godowns – buildings that served as both warehouses and office space. Such buildings were shared by traders and missionaries, such as the 1932 **China Baptist Publication Society**, whose Gothamesque offices at No 187 were designed by Ladislaus Hudec.

❼ Lyceum Building

Other restored buildings along this street include the **Lyceum Building** (1927), the multidenominational **Missions Building** (1924; No 169), the lovely **YWCA Building** (1932; No 133) and the red-brick **Yuanmingyuan Apartments** (No 115).

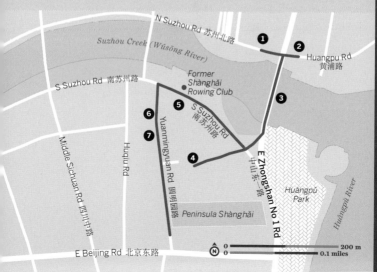

Best Walks
French Concession

🏃 The Walk

The French Concession's leafy backstreets and rich architectural diversity provide much inspiration for walks. The area is much more residential than the Bund and hence more conducive to leisurely strolls; there are also plenty of tiny boutiques to keep shoppers happy.

Start All Saints Church; **M** Xintiandi

Finish Cathay Theatre; **M** South Shaanxi Rd

Length 2.5km; 1½ hours

✕ Take a Break

Boxing Cat Brewery (拳击猫啤酒屋; Quánjīmāo Píjiǔwū; unit 26a, Sinan Mansions, 519 Middle Fuxing Rd; 复兴中路519号思南公馆26a; ⏰11am-2am; **M** Xintiandi) in the Sinan Mansions complex on Middle Fuxing Rd isn't as popular as its West Fuxing Rd outfit, but it's a staple among Shànghǎi's beer-o-philes, with a strong showing of craft brews.

KARL JOHANENGES / LOOK-FOTO / GETTY ©

French Concession (p60)

❶ All Saints Church

Begin the tour on Middle Fuxing Rd, first passing the red-brick Italianate **All Saints Church** (1925) and then the **Park Apartments** (1926) and smaller private villas fronted by large palm trees, from the same era.

❷ Former Residence of Liu Haisu

On Middle Fuxing Rd at No 512 is the **Former Residence of Liu Haisu** (1896–1994), a 20th-century artist who revolutionised traditional Chinese art by introducing Western painting styles.

❸ Dubail Apartment Building

The **Dubail Apartment Building** (1931) was the one-time home of US journalist and communist sympathiser Agnes Smedley (1892–1950). Smedley reported extensively on the Chinese civil war in the '30s.

❹ Sinan Mansions

This complex consists of 1920s private villas

that were built south of French Park (now Fùxīng Park); it was recently renovated as an upscale lifestyle destination. Today it houses cafes and restaurants, plus ultra-exclusive short-term residences to the south.

❺ Sun Yatsen's Former Residence

A short walk south on Sinan Rd (rte Massenet) is **Zhou Enlai's Former Residence** (No 73), which served primarily as the Communist Party's Shànghǎi office.

Retrace your footsteps along leafy Sinan Rd and its lovely stretch of old villas to reach **Sun Yatsen's Former Residence** (p68), where the father of modern China lived from 1918 to 1924.

❻ Russian Orthodox Mission Church

On Gaolan Rd (rte Cohen) is the **Russian Orthodox Mission Church**, built in 1934 and dedicated to Tsar Nicholas II.

❼ Nanchang Road

Nanchang Road (rue Vallon) is a popular shopping strip, with a number of fashion boutiques and antiques stores.

❽ Cathay Theatre

Maoming Road (rte Cardinal Mercier) is a shopping hot spot that specialises in tailored *qípáo* (气泡; cheongsams) and other Chinese-style clothes. Across busy Middle Huaíhai Rd is the 1932 **Cathay Theatre**, still in use as a movie theatre.

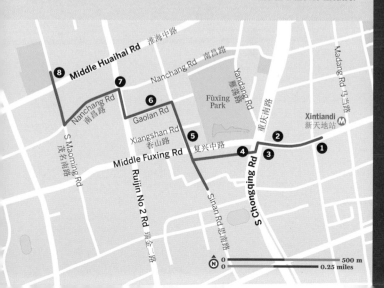

Best
Architecture

MARCO BRIVIO / GETTY IMAGES ©

Shànghǎi's sense of self as an erstwhile Paris of the East is inseparable from its architecture. The city is a treasure chest of architectural styles: Buddhist temple architecture, concession-era villas, homey alleyway houses, grandiose baroque banks, art deco apartment blocks, postmodern towers and dramatic skyscrapers topped with weird sci-fi protuberances. Whatever style floats your boat, Shànghǎi has it.

Lǐlòng & Shíkùmén

The Shànghǎi equivalent of Běijīng's charming *hútòng* alleyways and courtyard houses are its *lǐlòng* alleys (also called *lòngtáng*) and low-rise *shíkùmén* (石库门; stone-gate houses).

A distinctive blend of East and West, *shíkùmén* houses married the traditional Chinese courtyard house – with its interior courtyard features and emphasis on natural light – with the neat brickwork rows of English terrace housing.

Modern Architecture

Since the 1980s architects have been refashioning Shànghǎi's skyline in a bold way. The dramatic and modern Pǔdōng skyline, along with parts of Pǔxī, is testament to the newfound optimism and confidence that define the city. Edifices such as the Shànghǎi Tower reflect this resurgence, which has completely transformed the architectural heritage of Shànghǎi in under two decades.

Best Shíkùmén & Lǐlòng Architecture

Bubbling Well Road Apartments Great for everyday Shànghǎi life. (p96)

Tiánzǐfáng Charming alleyway complex bursting with shops and cafes. (p62)

Xīntiāndì Shànghǎi's traditional architectural vernacular re-imagined. (p64)

Best Modern Buildings

Shànghǎi Tower Pǔdōng's, Shànghǎi's and China's tallest tower. (p107)

Shànghǎi World Financial Center Distinctive bottle-opener-shaped tower in Pǔdōng. (p107)

China Art Palace, principal architect He Jingtang

Jīnmào Tower Eye-catching 88-storey skyscraper in Pǔdōng, designed by Adrian Smith. (pictured top left; p108)

Shànghǎi Grand Theatre State-of-the-art concert venue. (p44)

Best Historic Residences

Sun Yatsen's Former Residence Sun Yatsen lived here from 1918 to 1924. (p68)

Ba Jin's Former Residence Like something straight from the London suburbs. (p79)

Song Qingling's Former Residence Madame Sun Yatsen's residence after the foundation of

the People's Republic of China. (p79)

Mao Zedong's Former Residence Where young Mao lived in 1924. (p97)

Best Art Deco Buildings

Fairmont Peace Hotel An art deco landmark. (p44)

Rockbund Art Museum A winning blend of Chinese and art deco architectural styles. (p36)

Park Hotel With a fabulous art deco foyer. (p33)

Bank of China Art deco design meets Chinese sensibilities. (p25)

 Worth a Trip

Once the China Pavilion, the **China Art Palace** (中华艺术宫; Zhōnghuá Yìshùgōng; 205 Shangnan Rd; 上南路205号; admission free; ⏰9am-5pm Tue Sun; Ⓜ China Art Museum), opened as the city's new home of modern art. The **Power Station of Art** (上海当代艺术博物馆; Shànghǎi Dāngdài Yìshù Bówùguǎn; Lane 20, Huayuangang Rd; admission free; ⏰9am-5pm Tue-Sun; Ⓜ South Xizang Rd), stages more adventurous and thought-provoking exhibitions.

Best
Temples & Churches

To be spellbound by Shànghǎi's consumer madness is to ignore much of what modern China is about. To get a feel for the Chinese, it's vital to have an understanding of their devotional impulses. Religious observance has enjoyed a renaissance in Shànghǎi and the rest of China since 'opening up' took hold in the late 1970s.

BRYAN MULLENNIX / GETTY IMAGES ©

Christianity

China has a long history of importing faiths (Buddhism, Judaism, Islam, Christianity), but Christianity is making the most converts among modern Chinese. Proselytising is banned, but legions continue to turn to Christianity – partly because associations are made between the religion and the developed-world status of many Christian nations.

Buddhism

Buddhism has also enjoyed a considerable upsurge in the past decade, and constitutes the majority of worshippers in Shànghǎi. The best way to encounter religious observance is to visit the city's temples, such as Jìng'ān Temple or Jade Buddha Temple.

Best Temples

Jade Buddha Temple
Shànghǎi's most famous Buddhist temple, named after its sublime effigy. (p92)

Chénxiānggé Nunnery
Gorgeous temple in the Old Town. (p52)

Jìng'ān Temple Both the oldest and newest temple in Shànghǎi. (p100)

Confucius Temple
Peaceful shrine to the dictum-coining sage in an absorbing neighbourhood. (p55)

Temple of the Town God Revamped Taoist shrine a few steps from the Yùyuán Bazaar. (p51)

Best Churches

Hongkew Methodist Church Where Song Meiling (May-ling) married Chiang Kaishek in 1927. (p47)

Catholic Church Tiny single-steeple church in Qībǎo, dating to 1867 and attached to a convent. (p113)

Best
Views

An increasingly vertical city, Shànghǎi has some fabulous perches looking out onto classic panoramas. From snazzy high-rise bars to restaurants-with-a-view, the city is well supplied with window tables, but you may have to book ahead at certain spots to secure a seat.

WIN INITIATIVE / NEELEMAN / GETTY IMAGES ©

Best Hotel Views

Park Hyatt (柏悦酒店; Bóyuè Jiǔdiàn; www.parkhyattshanghai.com; Shànghǎi World Financial Center, 100 Century Ave; 世纪大道100号世界金融中心; **M**Lujiazui) Awesome panoramas, as standard.

Ritz-Carlton Shanghai Pudong Beyond the knockout design, the views are breathtaking. (p143)

Peninsula Hotel Five-star comfort, five-star views. (p143)

Best Bar Views

Flair Supremely high al fresco seats in Pǔdōng, with knockout views. (p111)

Sir Elly's Terrace Wow-factor visuals Bund-side. (p42)

Cloud 9 (九重天酒廊; Jiǔchóngtiān Jiǔláng; ☎021

5049 1234; 87th fl, Jinmao Tower, 88 Century Ave; 世纪大道88号金茂大厦87楼; ⏱5pm-1am Mon-Fri, 11am-2am Sat & Sun; **M**Lujiazui) Although indoors, Cloud 9 gives Flair a run for its money.

New Heights The definitive angle on Pǔdōng's glowing evening skyline. (p42)

Char Bar Chilled-out spot for electrifying evening visuals of Pǔdōng and the Bund. (p58)

Best Restaurant Views

South Beauty Grab a seat on the terrace for a mouth-watering panorama. (p110)

M on the Bund Supreme views of the Bund and Pǔdōng. (p40)

On 56 (意庐; Yìlú; ☎021 5047 1234; 54th-56th fl, Grand Hyatt, Jinmao Tower,

88 Century Ave; 世纪大道88号君悦大酒店; ⏱11.30am-2.30pm & 5.30-10.30pm; **M**Lujiazui) The swish selection of restaurants at the Grand Hyatt all come with breathtaking vistas.

Mercato A stylish spot with romantic Bund views. (p41)

Best Observation Decks

Shànghǎi Tower Lording it over Pǔdōng, with the world's highest observation deck. (p107)

Shànghǎi World Financial Center For many years home to the city's highest deck, now in second place. (pictured above; p107)

Jīnmào Tower Head up in the elevators to the 88th-floor observation deck for fantastic views. (p108)

Best **Museums & Galleries**

CHRISTIAN KOBER / GETTY IMAGES ©

Shànghǎi devotes considerably more time and energy to fulfilling large infrastructure projects than to nurturing a vibrant creative scene, but give the city credit for at least being halfway there: the number of new museums continues to grow each year. Even if you've been to Shànghǎi before, you'll always have plenty of exhibits to choose from.

Museums

The landmark cultural institution is the Shànghǎi Museum (p28), which contains one of the best collections of traditional art in the country. But don't overlook some of the smaller museums or the newer temples to modern art, where you'll get a feel for current social and artistic trends.

Galleries

Like many things in Shànghǎi, Chinese art is a commodity being increasingly vacuumed up by wealthy investors and foreign art hunters. Before you assume there's a genuine artistic revolution out there, it's worth noting the tendency for gallery-hung Chinese art to absorb Western needs and expectations like a multicoloured sponge. However, it also means that Shànghǎi is hardly short of galleries – head to M50 for the best.

☑ Top Tips

▶ Galleries and public museums are generally free.

▶ Many museums close their ticket offices 30 to 60 minutes before the venue itself closes.

▶ Students and seniors over 65 are sometimes eligible for discounted admission; take ID.

Best Art Museums

Shànghǎi Museum
Simply put, Shànghǎi's best museum. (p28)

Rockbund Art Museum
Top-notch contemporary art venue. (p36)

Liúlí China Museum
Glass sculpture, from

Shànghǎi Propaganda Poster Art Centre (p81)

2000-year-old jewellery to modern creations. (p63)

Shànghǎi Museum of Contemporary Art (MOCA Shànghǎi) Set in People's Park. (p38)

Shànghǎi Arts & Crafts Museum Shows crafts such as embroidery and paper-cutting. (p81)

Best Small Museums

Shànghǎi Urban Planning Exhibition Hall Idealised model layout of the city c 2020. (pictured top left; p36)

Shànghǎi History Museum Fun, interactive museum. (p108)

Shíkùmén Open House Museum See a restored *shíkùmén* (石库门; stonegate) house. (p65)

Shànghǎi Post Museum Postal history in imperial China. (p47)

Best Art Galleries

ShanghART One of Shànghǎi's longest-running galleries. (p95)

Power Station of Art Thought-provoking exhibitions in a humongous industrial space. (p121)

island6 Art collective producing multimedia installations. (p95)

Shànghǎi Propaganda Poster Art Centre Chinese socialist art from the 1950s, '60s and '70s. (p81)

m97 Photography with an emphasis on China-based artists. (p95)

Worth a Trip

Built in 1927 by the Russian Ashkenazi Jewish community, the **Ohel Moishe Synagogue** (摩西会堂; Móxī Huìtáng; 62 Changyang Rd; 长阳路62号; admission ¥50; ⊙9am-5pm, last entry 4.30pm; Ⓜ Dalian Rd) lies in the heart of the 1940s Jewish ghetto. Today it houses the Shànghǎi Jewish Refugees Museum, with exhibitions on the lives of the Central European refugees who fled to Shànghǎi to escape the Nazis.

Best
Boutiques

The Shanghainese have spent the past few years pounding nails into communism's coffin with a vengeance. 'Shop, shop, shop' has become the unofficial mantra, as everyone, from trendy 20-somethings to store-minding grandmothers, makes up for lost time. All the better for visitors: Shànghǎi shopping has never been so good.

Fashion

The French Concession's boutiques are the most interesting, though given the number of tiny shops, it can be hard to separate the wheat from the chaff. Start with strips such as Xinle Rd (a good variety of local fashion) and Nanchang Rd (good for browsing shoes, antiques and clothing). Changle Rd has a string of showrooms for up-and-coming designers.

Traditional Chinese Clothing

If you're in the market for a traditional Chinese jacket or *qípáo* (旗袍; traditional embroidered silk dress), you have plenty of tailors to choose from. South Maoming Rd just south of Huaihai Rd is a good place to compare designs and patterns; Shànghǎi 1936 (p63) at Tiánzǐfáng is another dependable choice.

Ceramics & Handicrafts

Although Chinese porcelain spent much of the 20th century in an artistic funk, a new generation of designers has started picking up the slack, trying to restore artistic credibility to Jǐngdézhèn ceramics. The results are on display in Shànghǎi's shops – look for everything from modernist teapots and dinnerware sets to exquisite handmade cups.

KYLIE McLAUGHLIN / GETTY IMAGES ©

☑ Top Tips

▶ Most shops are open from 10am to 10pm daily, though smaller boutiques may not open until noon.

Best Boutiques

Tiánzǐfáng More shops than you could ever visit in one day. (p62)

NuoMi Gorgeous dresses made from eco-friendly fabrics, including organic cotton and silk. (p88)

Lolo Love Vintage Fun and funky shop for all your vintage-frock needs. (p88)

OOAK Concept Boutique Three floors of inspiring jewellery, eye-catching modern women's clothing, bags and shoes. (p88)

Sūzhōu Cobblers (p45)

Best Ceramics

Spin New-wave, invigorating ceramics, from kung fu vases to oblong teacups. (p103)

Pīlìngpālāng Seriously funky and good-looking deco ceramics, cloisonné and lacquer. (p87)

Blue Shànghǎi White Small but exquisite collection of hand-painted ceramics. (p45)

Jǐngdézhèn Porcelain Artware High-quality traditional Chinese porcelain. (p97)

Huìfēng Tea Shop Quality Yixing teapots and loose-leaf tea. (p75)

Best Local Fashion

Xīntiāndì Shànghǎi-style haute couture, from local brands such as la vie and Woo. (p74)

Urban Tribe Established eco-conscious label with a lovely tea garden out the back. (p89)

Annabel Lee Peruse the collection of shawls, scarves, bags and table runners, most of which feature hand-stitched embroidery. (p45)

Madame Mao's Dowry Retro motifs and designer clothing. (p89)

Best Jewellery & Handicrafts

Amy Lin's Pearls High-quality salt- and freshwater pearls at unbeatable prices. (pictured top left; p103)

Brocade Country Charming collection of handicrafts from China's southwest. (p88)

Yúnwúxīn Exquisite line of handmade Tibetan-themed jewellery. (p74)

Sūzhōu Cobblers Hand-embroidered silk slippers. (p45)

Shànghǎi Arts & Crafts Museum All manner of handicrafts for sale, including fantastic paper cuts and Chinese lanterns. (p81)

Best
Markets &
Antiques

For variety and the best deals, roll up your sleeves at Shànghǎi's markets. Whether you're looking for tailor-made clothes, bargain T-shirts or a pet cricket, nothing can beat the sensory overload of a local market. You'll need pointy elbows and haggling is the norm, so make sure you test the waters before making a purchase, or you could pay over-the-top prices.

MARKA / GETTY IMAGES ©

Tailor-Made Clothes

The Old Town fabric markets have all manner of textiles, from synthetic to silk and cashmere – compare fabric and prices at different stands to ensure it's the real deal. Suits, pants, shirts, dresses and scarves can be made in as little as 24 hours (expect to pay extra), though a one-week turnaround is more realistic.

Counterfeits

'In Shànghǎi, everything can be faked except for your mother', or so the saying goes. Counterfeit goods are ubiquitous and there's no guarantee that you'll get the genuine item you're after. Antiques in particular are almost always reproductions: the best advice is to buy something because you like it, not because you think it has historic value.

Haggling

In the markets, haggling over prices is all part of the shopping experience. In particularly touristy places, you can usually get the price to drop by at least 50%, and sometimes even 75%.

☑ **Top Tips**

▶ Technically, nothing over 200 years old can be taken out of China, but you'll be very lucky if you come across any antiques that old in Shànghǎi. If you are buying a reproduction, make sure the dealer provides paperwork stating that it is not an antique.

Shíliùpù Fabric Market (p53)

Best Antiques

Old Street Excellent range of souvenirs, such as reproduced calendar posters. (p53)

Art Deco Stylish period furnishings that match the Fairmont Peace Hotel's streamlined aplomb. (p103)

Fúyòu Antique Market This place is at its best during the weekend 'ghost market'. (pictured top left; p53)

Best Clothing Markets

Shíliùpù Fabric Market Cashmere coats, silk shirts and dresses tailor-made for a song. (p53)

Han City Fashion & Accessories Plaza Scavenge for bargain bags, T-shirts, pearls and more. (p103)

Qīpǔ Market The go-to market for the lowest prices in town. (p47)

Best Traditional Markets

Fúyòu Antique Market Antiques, bric-a-brac and wares from the countryside. (p53)

Tanggu Road Food Market Live crabs and fish, pickled vegetables, mangoes, lychees and thousand-year-old eggs. (p47)

Best **Entertainment**

Shànghǎi is no longer the city of sin that went out dancing as the revolution made its way into town, but its entertainment options have blossomed once more over the past decade. Plug into the local cultural scene for a stimulating shot of jazz concerts, acrobatics or traditional Chinese music.

LONELY PLANET / GETTY IMAGES ©

Acrobatics

Shànghǎi troupes are among the best in the world and spending a night watching them spinning plates on poles and contorting themselves into unfeasible anatomical positions never fails to entertain. See www.shanghaiacrobaticshow.com for an overview of performances around town.

Music

Shànghǎi had a brief heyday in the jazz spotlight in the 1920s and '30s, when big-band swing was the entertainment of choice. It remains a popular genre and even if you won't catch many household names, there are some surprisingly good musicians here.

☑ Top Tips

▶ Tickets for all of the city's performing-arts events can be purchased at the venues where the performances take place; also check www.smartshanghai. com/smartticket.

Best Local Entertainment

Shànghǎi Centre Theatre Acrobatics performances. (pictured above; p102)

Bandu Cabin Traditional Chinese music performances on Saturday. (p102)

Shànghǎi Circus World Ever-popular show *Era:*

Intersection of Time combines acrobatics with new-fangled multi-media elements. (p137)

Yìfū Theatre Catch a Běijīng opera highlights show here. (p44)

Shànghǎi Grand Theatre From musicals and international orchestras to dance and theatre. (p44)

Best Rock & Jazz

Fairmont Peace Hotel Jazz Bar Featuring Shànghǎi's most famous jazz band. (p44)

MAO Livehouse The city's largest venue for rock and indie concerts. (p74)

Cotton Club The longest-running jazz and blues bar in Shànghǎi. (p87)

JZ Club Jazz bar showcasing a wide range of styles, from big band to groove. (p87)

Best
Massage & Spas

In Shànghǎi, a body or foot massage will come at a fraction of the price that you'd pay at home. Options range from neighbourhood foot-massage parlours – where everyone kicks back on an armchair and watches TV – to midrange and luxury hotel spas, which offer private rooms, a change of clothes and a wonderfully soothing atmosphere.

XPACIFICA / GETTY IMAGES ©

Dragonfly (悠庭保健会所; Yōutíng Bǎojiàn Huìsuǒ; ✆021 5403 9982; www.dragonfly.net.cn; 206 Xinle Road; 新乐路206号; ⏰10am-2am; Ⓜ South Shaanxi Rd) One of the longest-running massage services in Shànghǎi, the soothing Dragonfly offers Chinese body massages, foot massages and Japanese-style shiatsu (¥188 per 60 minutes), in addition to more specialised services such as hot-stone massages (whole body ¥580) and beauty treatments. Prices include a private room and a change of clothes. Reserve.

Peninsula Hotel
Located just steps from the Bund, the **Peninsula Spa** (⏰11am-midnight Mon-Fri, 10am-midnight Sat-Sun) is an indulgent and beautiful choice, elegantly styled with a 1930s Chinese deco theme, providing his-and-hers thermal suites and the full range of Oriental pampering and therapies. (p143)

Green Massage (青籁养身; Qīnglài Yǎngshén; ✆021 5386 0222; www.green-massage.com.cn; 58 Taicang Rd; 太仓路58号; massages & spa treatments ¥198-318; ⏰10.30am-2am; Ⓜ South Huangpi Rd) Calming fragrances envelop guests at this plush midrange spa, which offers foot, *tuīná* (推拿; traditional) and shiatsu massages. In addition to traditional practices such as cupping and moxibustion, it also provides waxing and other beauty treatments. There's also a **Jìng'ān branch** (✆021 6289 7776; 2nd fl, Shànghǎi Centre, 1376 West Nanjing Rd; 南京西路1376号2楼; ⏰10.30am-2am; Ⓜ Jing'an Temple, West Nanjing Rd). Reserve.

Double Rainbow Massage House (双彩虹保健按摩厅; Shuāng Cǎihóng Bǎojiàn Ànmó Tīng; 45 Yongjia Rd; 永嘉路45号; massage ¥68; ⏰noon-midnight; Ⓜ South Shaanxi Rd) Perhaps Shànghǎi's best neighbourhood massage parlour, the visually impaired masseuses here will have you groaning in agony in no time as they seek out those oft-neglected pressure points. The rates are a steal.

Best
Food

Shànghǎi is the white-hot crucible of China's economic alchemy, and the fizzing sense of excitement also fires up its kitchens. The city is as much a magnet for regional Chinese chefs as it is for superstar toques from around the globe, and has staked a formidable claim as the Middle Kingdom's trendiest dining destination.

ZOOM-ZOOM / GETTY IMAGES ©

Shanghainese

Don't come to Shànghǎi without sampling its celebrated local cuisine, which is generally sweeter than other Chinese cuisines. Standout dishes include braised pork belly (红烧肉; *hóngshāo ròu*), drunken chicken (醉鸡; *zuì jī*), smoked fish (熏鱼; *xūn yú*) and the local dumpling varieties: *xiǎolóngbāo* (小笼包; steamed or soup dumplings) and *shēngjiān* (生煎; fried dumplings).

Regional Chinese

China's flavours converge in Shànghǎi. You don't have to trek to far-flung Kashgar for Uighur noodles or Húnán for Mao's stewed pork. Don't be afraid to experiment – and do as the Shanghainese do: dig in with those chopsticks!

Best Shanghainese

Jian Guo 328 A tight squeeze but also crammed with flavour. (p83)

Jesse Shanghainese home cooking in all its sweet, oily glory. (p83)

Fu 1039 Old-fashioned charm and succulent Shanghainese. (p84)

Yè Shànghǎi Elegant presentation and 1930s decor. (p72)

Lynn Ever-popular Jing'ān choice with a surefire menu. (p101)

☑ Top Tips

▶ Tipping is not done in the majority of restaurants. High-end international restaurants are another matter: while tipping is not obligatory, it is encouraged.

▶ Plenty of places have English and/or picture menus.

▶ Reserve a few days in advance for more popular restaurants.

Best Regional Chinese

Dī Shuǐ Dòng Countryside cookin' and Hunanese chilli peppers. (p70)

Shànghǎi Grandmother Fantastic dishes from

Nánxiáng Steamed Bun Restaurant (p58)

all over China, near the Bund. (p39)

Lost Heaven Trendy Yunnanese specialities. (p38)

Cha's Travel back in time to a 1950s Hong Kong diner. (p70)

Best Dumplings

Din Tai Fung Sophisticated Taiwanese street food. (p70)

Yang's Fry Dumplings Simple, greasy and great. (p41)

Nánxiáng Steamed Bun Restaurant The oldest *xiǎolóngbāo* chain in Shànghǎi. (p58)

Yunnan Road Food Street Shaanxi dumplings, cold noodles, five-fragrance dim sum and more. (p41)

Crystal Jade Great for Singapore- and Shànghǎi-style dim sum. (p71)

Best Vegetarian

Vegetarian Lifestyle Hip, delicious and organic. (p101)

Jade Buddha Temple Vegetarian Restaurant Eat with monks and nuns. (p93)

Sōngyuèlóu Shànghǎi's oldest veggie restaurant. (p58)

Best Gastronomic

Mr & Mrs Bund Re-imagined French bistro fare for night owls. (p40)

Commune Social Seriously neat Jason Atherton operation in Jìng'ān. (p100)

M on the Bund The grande dame of Shànghǎi dining. (p40)

T8 *Shíkùmén* setting and Sìchuān high pie. (p70)

Best Street Food

Qībǎo Poke a straw in a coconut and chomp on barbecued squid. (p112)

Yunnan Road Food Street One of the best strips for unpretentious regional Chinese restaurants. (p41)

Wujiang Road Food Street The most modern snack street in the city, stuffed with options. (p102)

Yùyuán Gardens & Bazaar Crowded and overpriced, but loads of good snacking options at stalls and in restaurants. (p50)

Best
Drinking

Shànghǎi adores its lychee martinis and flat whites to go, and with dazzling salaries and soaring property prices leaving the streets awash with cash, there are more than enough bars and cafes to water the thirsty white-collar set. Don't be intimidated by the glitzy exterior: there's a happening nightlife scene that keeps everyone – VIP or not – well entertained.

LONELY PLANET / GETTY IMAGES ©

Bars

Shànghǎi has stayed true to its roots: it's all about looking flash, sipping craft cocktails or imported wine, and tapping into the insatiable appetite for new trends. New bars pop up and disappear in a blink, but the upside to the competition is that weekly specials and happy hours (generally from 5pm to 8pm) help keep the city affordable.

Cafes

Cafe culture has long steeped Shànghǎi in caffeine. Though you'd be hard-pressed to find a decent teahouse within a 20km radius, lattes and sandwiches served at hip wireless hangouts are all over the place. Another common sight is street stalls selling Taiwanese bubble tea, and all sorts of related spin-offs, such as hot ginger drinks or papaya smoothies.

Clubbing

Shànghǎi's clubs are mostly big, glossy places devoted to playing mainstream house, techno and hip-hop. A number of big-name DJs have helped boost interest among locals, although the crowds are still mainly made up of Westerners, Hong Kong and Taiwanese expats, and young, rich Shanghainese. Check local listings for the latest hot spots.

☑ **Top Tips**

► Many bars offer a full dining menu and open for lunch at 11am. Bars that only serve drinks are more erratic; they might open anywhere between 4.30pm and 8pm. Last call is between 2am and 5am.

► Clubs generally don't get going until 10pm and stay open until 5am on weekends.

Barbarossa (p43)

Best Design

Long Bar Colonial-era decor and old-fashioned cocktails. (p42)

Old Shànghǎi Teahouse For a taste of 1930s Shànghǎi. (p53)

Bar Rouge Chic Bund lounge, with electro beats and ruby-red lighting. (pictured top left; p42)

Apartment Hip bar with drinks, dining and dancing. (p84)

Barbarossa Escape to this oasis in People's Park. (p43)

Best Cocktails

Sir Elly's Terrace Thrilling al fresco views, stunning drinks. (p42)

El Cóctel Retro cocktail lounge with perfectionist barkeeps. (p84)

Fennel Lounge Sunken bar, live music and a grown-up vibe. (p86)

Best for Beer

Boxing Cat Brewery Much-applauded three-storey microbrewery. (p118)

Dean's Bottle Shop Great range, low prices. (p73)

Kāibā Shànghǎi's imported-beer specialist. (p63)

Shànghǎi Brewery Gargantuan microbrewery with dining, and live sports on TV. (p86)

Cafe des Stagiaires Brimful of zany Gallic charm. (p72)

Best Cafes

Sumerian Small place, packed with flavour. (p100)

Café 85°C Sea-salt coffee and frothy green tea. (p97)

Wagas Shànghǎi's own wi-fi-equipped cafe chain. (p100)

Best Clubs

Shelter Underground beats in an old bomb shelter. (p85)

M1nt This exclusive penthouse lounge is the ultimate see-and-be-seen destination. (p44)

Best
Taichi & Martial Arts

Dreaming of upending hardened karate fourth-dan black belts with a mere shrug? Itching to master the devastating eight palm changes of Bāguà Zhǎng? Now is your chance. For many young Chinese, learning martial arts is about as sexy as watching paint dry, but the mind-bending antics of Bruce Lee and Jackie Chan have fired up generations of eager Westerners.

BEN PIPE PHOTOGRAPHY / GETTY IMAGES ©

Good places to look for teachers and students are Shànghǎi's parks, first thing in the morning. If you ask to join a group of practitioners, you'll usually be welcomed.

Lóngwǔ Kung Fu Center (龙武功夫馆;
Lóngwǔ Gōngfu Guǎn; ☏ 021 6287 1528; www.longwukungfu.com; 1 South Maoming Rd; 茂名南路1号; 1-/2-/3-month lesson ¥100/450/700; **M** South Shaanxi Rd) Coaches from Shànghǎi's martial-arts teams give classes in Chinese, Japanese and Korean martial arts. The largest centre in the city, it also offers children's classes on weekend mornings and lessons in English.

Wǔyì Chinese Kungfu Centre (武懿国术馆;
Wǔyì Guóshù Guǎn; ☏ 137 0168 5893; room 311, 3rd fl, International Artists' Factory, No 3, Lane 210, Taikang Rd; 法租界泰康路210弄3号3楼311; **M** Dapuqiao) English-language taichi classes on Thursday and Sunday and wǔshù (武术) classes on Wednesday and Sunday for adults and kids.

Míngwǔ International Kungfu Club (明武国际功夫馆; Míngwǔ Guójì Gōngfu Guǎn; ☏ 021 6465 9806; www.mingwukungfu.com; 3rd fl, Hongchun Bldg, 3213 Hongmei Rd; 虹梅路3213号红春大厦3楼; ⛹) This versatile gym offers bilingual classes in a wide range of martial arts, from taichi and qìgōng (气功) to wǔshù and karate, for both children and adults.

Best
For Kids

Shànghǎi isn't on most kids' holiday radars, but the new Shànghǎi Disney Resort in Pǔdōng (open in spring 2016) will no doubt improve this situation. Beyond this, there are plenty of sights that will keep the family entertained.

Also check out these possibilities online: Happy Valley (sh.happyvalley.cn), Dino Beach (www.64783333.com), Shànghǎi Science & Technology Museum (p110) and the Shànghǎi Ocean Aquarium (www.sh-aquarium.com). Bus tours are a good option for getting around the city with kids.

Shànghǎi World Financial Center Ascend supersonic elevators to the sky-high observation decks. (p107)

Shànghǎi Tower Home to the world's highest observation deck when it opens in 2015/16. (p107)

Shànghǎi History Museum Wax figures and interactive exhibits make this a family-friendly museum. (p108)

Shànghǎi Centre An evening of plate-spinning and contortionism never fails to entertain. (p102)

Shànghǎi Circus World (上海马戏城; Shànghǎi Mǎxìchéng; ☎ 021 6652 7501; www.era-shanghai. com/era/en/; 2266 Gonghexin Rd; 共和新路 2266号; admission ¥120-600; Ⓜ Shanghai Circus World) Eye-popping acrobatics, gymnastics and motorcyclists show.

Shànghǎi Maglev Super fast, say no more. (pictured above; p144)

XPACIFICA / GETTY IMAGES ©

☑ **Top Tips**

▶ In general, 1.4m is the cut-off height for children's tickets. Children under 0.8m normally get in for free.

▶ The popularity of kids' attractions everywhere peaks on holidays and at weekends, but in China, 'crowded' takes on a new meaning. Try to schedule your visits for weekdays if possible.

Best
For Free

KARL JOHAENTGES / LOOK-FOTO / GETTY IMAGES ©

With prices constantly rising, Shànghǎi is China's most expensive city, bar Hong Kong, but there are a few tips for getting more for your máo.

Cheap Eats

Shànghǎi's restaurant prices are high when compared to the rest of China, and to top it off, portions are smaller. Malls are always a good place to find cheap eats; check the basement or top floors for food courts. Street food is another good bet – think dumpling stalls and noodle shops.

Some restaurants catering to office workers offer good-value weekday lunch specials: to take advantage, ask for a *tàocān* (套餐; set menu).

Film Screenings

A handful of bars and cafes around town screen weekly films for free. Check local mags for the monthly schedule.

Best Museums

Shànghǎi Museum
Simply put, Shànghǎi's best museum. (p28)

Shànghǎi Gallery of Art Neat and minimalist Bund art gallery for highbrow and conceptual Chinese art. (pictured above; interior renovation designed by Michael Graves Architecture & Design; p38)

M50 The largest complex of modern-art galleries in Shànghǎi. (p94)

Shànghǎi Post Museum Surprisingly interesting, with great views. (p47)

Best Communist Heritage

Site of the 1st National Congress of the CCP Certainly not the most enthralling attraction but a must for political-history buffs. Passport required. (p65)

Mao Zedong's Former Residence Traditional *shíkùmén* architecture and Mao memorabilia. Passport required. (p97)

Best
Green Spaces

JOHN NORMAN / ALAMY STOCK PHOTO ©

Although at first glance Shànghǎi seems to be as concrete as they come, with a little exploration you can find some pleasant acres of greenery and some attractively landscaped areas. Like the historic architecture, Shànghǎi's main parks are generally European in layout, though the flora is primarily native, with lots of magnolia trees, fatsia and bamboo.

The most central green space is People's Park, located on the northern half of People's Square. Built on the site of the colonial racetrack, the park is a leafy refuge in the heart of the city, and is home to a museum and pond-side cafe-bar. If you're in Shànghǎi in June, look out for the pink lotus flowers in the pond.

If you want to picnic on the grass or kick a football about, you're out of luck. Shànghǎi's modern parks are largely synthetically designed, with concrete trimming and recurrent 'keep-off-the-grass' notices. Larger parks include Shànghǎi Zoo and Zhōngshān Park in the west of town.

Fùxīng Park Once known as French Park, Fùxīng Park is an excellent spot for early-morning taichi classes. (pictured above; p68)

People's Park All-important enclave of greenery at the geographic heart of Shànghǎi. (p33)

Riverside Promenade This Pǔdōng walkway is lined with cafes and ice-cream stands. (p109)

Best
Tours

Best Bicycle Tours

BOHDI (☏021 5266 9013; www.bohdi.com.cn; tours ¥220) Night-time cycling tours on Tuesday (March to November) and trips out of town.

SISU (☏021 5059 6071; www.sisucycling.com; tours ¥150) Night-time cycling tours on Wednesday and trips out of town.

Best Boat Tours

Huángpǔ River Cruise – The Bund (黄浦江游览; Huángpǔ Jiāng Yóulǎn; 219-239 East Zhongshan No 2 Rd; 中山东二路 219-239号; tickets ¥128; MEast Nanjing Rd) Ninety-minute cruises run from the south end of the Bund (near East Jinling Rd) up to the International Cruise Terminal and back – and then they do it all over again. Try to find a rarer 40- to 60-minute cruise (¥100), which only makes the

trip once. Departure times vary, but cruises usually run from 11am to 8.30pm.

Huángpǔ River Cruise – Pǔdōng (黄浦江游览船, Huángpǔjiāng Yóulǎnchuán; Pearl Dock, 明珠码头; tickets ¥100; ☉10am-1.30pm; MLujiazui) Six 40-minute cruises depart hourly from Pǔdōng.

Best Bus & Motorcycle Tours

Big Bus Tours (上海观光车; Shànghǎi Guānguāngchē; ☏021 6351 5988; www.bigbustours.com; adult/child US$48/32) Hop-on, hop-off bus services lassoing in the top sights along 22 stops across two routes. Valid for 48 hours, tickets include a 90-minute boat tour of the Huángpǔ River, plus admission to the Jade Buddha Temple and the observation deck of Jīnmào Tower.

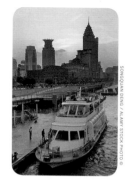

SONGQUAN DENG / ALAMY STOCK PHOTO ©

City Sightseeing Buses (都市观光; Dūshì Guānguāng; ☏400 820 6222; www.springtour.com; tickets ¥30; ☉9am-8.30pm summer, to 6pm winter) Tickets for these handy hop-on, hop-off, open-top bus tours last 24 hours. It's a convenient way to tour Shànghǎi's highlights and a great way to get around the centre of town and Pǔdōng.

Insiders Experience (☏138 1761 6975; www.insidersexperience.com; from ¥800) Unusual motorcycle-sidecar tours of the city for up to two passengers, setting off from the Andaz hotel in Xīntiāndì.

Survival Guide

Survival Guide

Before You Go

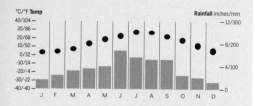

When to Go

°C/°F Temp
40/104 —
30/86 —
20/68 —
10/50 —
0/32 —
-10/14 —
-20/-4 —
-30/-22 —
-40/-40 —

Rainfall inches/mm
— 12/300
— 8/200
— 4/100
— 0

J F M A M J J A S O N D

➡ **Winter (Dec–Feb)**
Cold, clammy. Lunar New Year arrives with a bang in January or February.

➡ **Spring (Mar–May)**
Temperatures rise. Late April and May are pleasant, but avoid major holidays.

➡ **Summer (Jun–Aug)**
Rainfall in Shànghǎi hits its peak in June, as the sweltering summer heat arrives.

➡ **Autumn (Sep–Nov)**
This is one of the best times to visit, as temperatures drop.

Book Your Stay

☑ **Top Tip** Always take your hotel's business card with you when you go out for the day. You will need to show the Chinese address to your driver if you return via taxi.

➡ Shànghǎi's sleeping options are excellent at either end of the spectrum, though quality in the midrange market remains in short supply – do your homework and secure a room well ahead of time.

➡ Check out top-end hotels; competition and heavy discounts mean rates are often reasonable.

➡ Four- and five-star hotels add a 10% or 15% service charge (sometimes negotiable).

➡ Save money by staying at a Chinese chain (eg Motel 168) or in a private double in a hostel.

➡ Private doubles in hostels are cheaper (and often better) than rooms in locally run midrange hotels, and the level of service is much higher, as staff are sure to speak English.

➡ Most hotels have air-conditioning, broadband internet access and/or wi-fi.

Useful Websites

CTrip (english.ctrip.com) and **eLong** (www.elong.net) are both reliable sites for hotel and domestic-flight bookings.

Lonely Planet (www.lonelyplanet.com/hotels) Author-penned reviews and online booking.

Best Budget

Mingtown Nanjing Road Youth Hostel (明堂上海南京路青年旅舍) Sociable and friendly hostel located halfway between the Bund and People's Square.

Le Tour Traveler's Rest (乐途静安国际青年旅舍; www.letourshanghai.com) Hostel housed in a former towel factory with red-brick walls and repro stone gateways.

Mingtown E-Tour Youth Hostel (明堂上海青年旅舍) Choice location just behind People's Square; has a tranquil courtyard.

Mingtown Hiker Youth Hostel (明堂上海旅行者青年旅馆) Well-located dorms a short hop from the Bund.

Motel 168 (莫泰连锁旅馆; www.motel168.com) Modern doubles and the price is right.

Best Midrange

Astor House Hotel (浦江饭店; www.astorhousehotel.com) Fab location and superb old-world charm.

Quintet (www.quintetshanghai.com) Chic B&B with modern design.

Marvel Hotel (商悦青年会大酒店; www.marvelhotels.com.cn) Located in the former YMCA building off People's Square.

Magnolia Bed & Breakfast (www.magnoliabnbshanghai.com) Cosy B&B in a 1927 French Concession home.

Kevin's Old House (老时光酒店; www.kevinsoldhouse.com) Lovely French Concession boutique hotel with stylish suites.

Best Top End

Fairmont Peace Hotel (费尔蒙和平饭店; www.fairmont.com) The city's most famous hotel, renovated in all its art deco magic.

Langham Xīntiāndì (新天地朗廷酒店; www.langhamhotels.com) Top-of-the-line French Concession luxury.

Urbn (www.urbnhotels.com) China's first carbon-neutral hotel.

Ritz-Carlton Shanghai Pudong (上海浦东丽思卡尔顿酒店; www.ritzcarlton.com) Beautifully designed rooms with dramatic Bund-side views.

Peninsula Hotel (半岛酒店; www.peninsula.com) Spiffing blend of art deco motifs with Shànghǎi modernity.

Arriving in Shànghǎi

☑ **Top Tip** For the best way to get to your accommodation, see p17.

Pǔdōng International Airport

Pǔdōng International Airport (PVG; 浦东国际机场; Pǔdōng Guójì Jīchǎng; ☏ 021 6834 1000, flight information ☏ 96990; www.shairport.com) is 30km southeast of Shànghǎi, and handles all international flights. There are four ways to get from the airport to the city: Maglev train, taxi, metro and bus.

➡ The bullet-fast **Maglev** (磁浮列车; Cífú Lièchē; www.smtdc.com; economy one way/return ¥50/80, with same-day air ticket ¥40, children under/over 1.2m free/half price) takes eight minutes from Pǔdōng. Arriving at the terminus (Longyang Rd), transfer to metro line 2 or take a taxi into town. You should pay ¥40 to ¥60 to downtown Shànghǎi (People's Square) from Longyang Rd.

➡ A taxi ride from the airport to central Shànghǎi will cost around ¥160 (about an hour). Take a cab from the official taxi rank; make sure the meter is on.

➡ Metro line 2 runs to central Shànghǎi and is the cheapest way to get to town (¥7 to People's Square, 75 minutes). Switch trains (but not metro lines) at Guanglan Rd in Pǔdōng. Service to the airport runs from 6.30am to 9pm. For evening departures, be at Guanglan Rd by 9pm for the last metro to the airport.

➡ Buses run from the airport, taking between 60 and 90 minutes to destinations in central Shànghǎi. Buses leave the airport from 6.30am to 11pm; they go to the airport from 5.30am to 9.30pm (bus 1 runs till 11pm). The most useful buses are airport bus 1 (¥30), which links Pǔdōng International Airport with Hóngqiáo Airport (terminals 1 and 2), and airport bus 2 (¥22), which links Pǔdōng International Airport with the Airport City Terminal, east of Jìng'ān Temple.

Hóngqiáo Airport

Hóngqiáo Airport (SHA; 虹桥机场; Hóngqiáo Jīchǎng; ☏ 021 6268 8899) serves domestic destinations and is 18km west of the Bund, a 30- to 60-minute trip.

➡ Most flights now arrive at Terminal 2, which is connected to downtown via metro lines 2 and 10 (30 minutes to People's Square).

➡ If you arrive at Terminal 1, you can also catch the airport shuttle bus (¥4, operates between 7.50am and 11pm) to the Airport City Terminal, east of Jìng'ān Temple.

➡ Taxis cost ¥70 to ¥100 to central Shànghǎi and ¥200 to Pǔdōng International Airport.

Hóngqiáo Railway Station

Hóngqiáo Railway Station (上海虹桥站; Shànghǎi Hóngqiáo Zhàn) is adjacent to Hóngqiáo Airport. It's the terminus for the Shànghǎi–Běijīng high-speed G-class trains; express trains to Hángzhōu and Sūzhōu also leave from here. It is served by metro lines 2 and 10.

Shànghǎi Railway Station

Trains depart to destinations all over China from **Shànghǎi Railway Station** (上海火车站; Shànghǎi Huǒchē Zhàn; ☏ 021 6317 9090; 385 Meiyuan Rd). Trains from Hong Kong also arrive here. It is served by metro lines 1, 3 and 4.

Shànghǎi South Railway Station

Trains from southern destinations, such as Hángzhōu, arrive at **Shànghǎi South Railway Station** (上海南站; Shànghǎi Nánzhàn; ☏ 021 9510 5123; 200 Zhaofeng Rd). It is served by metro lines 1 and 3.

Getting Around

Metro
☑ **Best for...**
General travel throughout Shànghǎi.

➡ The city's metro, indicated by a large red M, is the best way to get around town. It is fast, cheap and clean, although it's often packed and it doesn't run late. With 14 lines serving 300 stations, it's among the world's longest metro systems.

➡ The most useful lines for travellers are 1, 2 and 10.

➡ Tickets range from ¥3 to ¥15, depending on distance; buy them from the bilingual automated machines. Keep your ticket until you exit.

➡ Most trains run from about 5.30am to 10.30pm.

Taxi
☑ **Best for...** Reaching destinations not located near metro stops, and for travelling after 10.30pm.

➡ Shànghǎi's taxis (出租车; chūzū chē) are reasonably cheap, hassle-free and easy to flag down outside rush hour, although finding a cab during rainstorms is impossible.

➡ Flag fall is ¥14 (for the first 3km) and ¥18 at night (11pm to 5am). For the most part, Shànghǎi's cabbies are honest, but make sure you can see the meter when you get in the car and that it is turned on.

➡ To overcome the language barrier, always take the Chinese address of your destination.

➡ If you feel you've been cheated, make sure you get a receipt and the cab driver's ID number, then call the company to file a complaint. Among the main taxi companies are **Bāshì** (巴士; ☏ 96840) and **Qiángshēng** (强生; ☏ 021 6258 0000).

Tickets & Passes

A one-/three-day metro pass is sold at the airports and from some information desks for ¥18/45. If you are going to be doing a lot of travelling in Shànghǎi, invest in a transport card (交通卡; jiāotōng kǎ). Sold at metro stations and some convenience stores, these handy cards can be filled up with credit and used on the metro and most buses and in taxis. The ¥20 deposit can be refunded at East Nanjing Rd metro station before you leave.

Essential Information

Business Hours

☑ **Top Tip** Final entry to many museums is generally half an hour to an hour before the official closing time.

➡ Banks are normally open from 9am to noon and about 2pm to 4.30pm Monday to Friday. Most banks have 24-hour ATMs. Some branches also open on Saturday morning.

➡ Restaurants are open from 11am to 10pm or later. Fancier places close for an afternoon break at about 2.30pm, before re-opening from 5pm to 11pm or later.

➡ Department stores are generally open from 10am to 10pm; smaller boutiques may not open until noon but generally stay open until 9pm or 10pm.

➡ Some bars open for lunch, others open at about 5pm. Last call is generally 2am, but there are a handful of places that stay open until dawn.

Discount Cards

➡ Students and seniors over the age of 65 often qualify for reduced admission. You will need to provide ID as proof.

Scams

'Hello, can you help us take a photo?' This ostensibly harmless question is in fact one of the better hooks for Shànghǎi's main scam. Young people posing as students work the main tourist drags – the Bund, East Nanjing Rd and the exit of the Shànghǎi Museum – engaging tourists in conversation. However the conversation starts, it inevitably ends with an invitation to a 'traditional tea ceremony' or 'art gallery'. Intrigued? Don't be. You'll wind up with a US$100 bill (or much more) and a private escort to the closest ATM.

Electricity

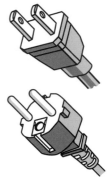

220V/50Hz

220V/50Hz

Emergency

Ambulance (☎120)

Fire (☎119)

Police (☎110)

Money

➡ The Chinese currency is known as rénmínbì (RMB). The basic unit of RMB is the yuán (¥). For updated currency exchange rates, check www.xe.com.

➡ It's easiest to use cash in Shànghǎi; ATMs that take foreign cards are widespread. Look for the Bank of China (中国银行), Industrial and Commercial Bank of China (ICBC; 工商银行) and HSBC (汇丰银行), many of which have 24-hour ATMs. Many top-end hotels, shopping malls and department stores also have ATMs.

➡ Most tourist hotels will accept major credit cards, as will banks, high-end restaurants and international boutiques.

Public Holidays

New Year's Day
1 January

Lunar New Year
28 January 2017, 16 February 2018; a week-long break, also known as Chinese New Year, or Spring Festival

Tomb Sweeping Day
First weekend in April; three-day weekend

International Labour Day 1 May; three-day weekend

Dragon Boat Festival 9 June 2016, 30 May 2017

Mid-Autumn Festival 15 September 2016, 4 October 2017

National Day 1 October; officially three days but often morphs into a week-long holiday

Safe Travel

➡ Shànghǎi feels very safe, and crimes against foreigners are rare. Crossing the road is probably the greatest danger.

➡ If any of your possessions are stolen, report the crime at the district Public Security Bureau (PSB; 公安局) office and obtain a police report.

Money-Saving Tips

➡ Many public museums are free.

➡ Aim to drink at bars during the ubiquitous happy hours, which generally run from 5pm to 8pm.

Telephone

☑ **Top Tip** Buy a cheap, unlocked GSM phone for international travel. Then simply buy a SIM card once you arrive at your destination and you're good to go.

Mobile Phones

➡ Inexpensive pay-as-you-go SIM cards are available for unlocked GSM phones. If your phone is not compatible (eg Verizon customers in the US), buying or renting a local phone may be a better option than international roaming plans.

➡ The main service providers are China Mobile (中国移动) and China Unicom (中国联通), both of which have sales counters at Pǔdōng International Airport (arrivals hall) and around Shànghǎi.

➡ You can buy SIM cards at some convenience stores and magazine kiosks; cheap phones can be found at electronics markets.

Shànghǎi Dos & Don'ts

➡ When presenting your business card, proffer it with the first finger and thumb of both hands (thumbs on top).

➡ Don't stick your chopsticks vertically into your rice; lay them down on your plate or on the chopstick rest.

➡ Always hand your cigarettes around in social situations.

➡ Don't insist on paying the dinner or bar bill if your fellow diner appears determined.

➡ 'Losing face' is about making people look stupid or forcing them to back down in front of others. Take care to avoid it and don't lose sight of your own face in the process.

➡ If you prefer to rent a mobile phone (you'll still need to buy a SIM card), you can get one at Pǔdōng International Airport or via www.pandaphone. com. It will probably cost about US$50 for a week, including all fees and the SIM card.

Country & City Codes
Note the following country and city codes; if calling Shànghǎi or Běijīng from abroad, drop the first zero.

➡ **People's Republic of China** (☎86)

➡ **Shànghǎi** (☎021)

➡ **Běijīng** (☎010)

Toilets
☑ **Top Tip** The golden rule is always to carry an emergency stash of toilet paper – many toilets are devoid of such essentials.

➡ Public toilets in Shànghǎi are numerous, but the quality of the experience varies greatly. In an emergency, look for a high-end hotel or a fast-food restaurant.

➡ Toilets in hotels are generally sitters, but expect to find squatters in many public toilets. In all but the cheapest hotels it's safe to flush toilet paper down the toilet. If you see a small waste-paper basket in the corner of the toilet, that is

where you should throw the toilet paper. Tampons always go in the basket.

➡ The Chinese characters for men and women are 男 (men) and 女 (women).

Tourist Information
☑ **Top Tip** Your hotel should be able to provide you with most of the tourist information you require. You can also pick up free maps of Shànghǎi and the metro at the airports.

Shànghǎi Call Centre (☎021 962 288) This toll-free English-language hotline is possibly the most useful telephone number in Shànghǎi – it can even give your cab driver directions via your mobile phone.

Shànghǎi Information Centre for International Visitors (Map p66, F2; ☎021 6384 9366; Xīntiāndì South Block, Bldg 2, Xingye Rd; ⏰10am-10pm) Xīntiāndì information centre with currency exchange and free brochures.

Tourist Information & Service Centres
The standard of English varies from good to nonexistent, though most branches have free maps.

Tourist Information & Service Centre (Map p34, G2; 旅游咨询服务中心; Lǚyóu Zīxún Fúwù Zhōngxīn) Bund-side tourist information and maps.

Tourist Information & Service Centre (Map p34, E3; 旅游咨询服务中心; Lǚyóu Zīxún Fúwù Zhōngxīn; ☏021 6357 3718; 518 Jiujiang Rd; 九江路518号; ☺9.30am-8pm)

Tourist Information & Service Centre (Map p80, C1; 旅游咨询服务中心; Lǚyóu Zīxún Fúwù Zhōngxīn; ☏021 6248 3259; Lane 1678, 18 West Nanjing Rd; 南京西路1678弄18号; ☺9am-5pm)

Tourist Information & Service Centre (Map p54, C2; 旅游咨询服务中心; Lǚyóu Zīxún Fúwù Zhōngxīn; ☏021 6355 5032; 149 Jiujiaochang Rd; 旧校场路149号; ☺9am-7pm) Southwest of Yùyuán Gardens.

Travellers with Disabilities

Shànghǎi's traffic and poor infrastructure are the greatest challenges to travellers with disabilities. Metro-system escalators don't go both ways. That said, an increasing number of modern buildings, museums, stadiums and most new hotels are wheelchair accessible.

Visas

☑ **Top Tip** Start your visa paperwork about a month before your trip.

Seventy-two-hour visa-free transits are allowed in Shànghǎi for citizens of many nations as long as they have visas for their onward destinations (departure point and destination point cannot be in the same country) and proof of seats booked on flights out of China. Otherwise, a visa is required for all visitors to China except for citizens of Japan, Singapore and Brunei. Visas can be obtained from Chinese embassies and consulates. Most tourists get a single-entry visa for a 30-day stay, valid for three months from the date of issue. Longer-stay multiple-entry visas also exist, though obtaining one can be more of a hassle – it all depends upon the current rules at your local embassy.

Your passport must be valid for at least six months after the expiry date of your visa; at least one entire blank page in your passport is required for the visa.

Language

Mandarin Chinese – or Pǔtōnghuà (common speech), as it's referred to by the Chinese – can be written using the Roman alphabet. This system is known as Pinyin; in the following phrases we have provided both Mandarin script and Pinyin.

Mandarin has 'tonal' quality – the raising and lowering of pitch on certain syllables. There are four tones in Mandarin, plus a fifth 'neutral' tone that you can all but ignore. In Pinyin the tones are indicated with accent marks on vowels: ā (high), á (rising), ǎ (falling-rising), à (falling).

To enhance your trip with a phrasebook, visit **lonelyplanet.com**.

Basics

Hello.	你好。	Nǐhǎo.
Goodbye.	再见。	Zàijiàn.
How are you?	你好吗？	Nǐhǎo ma?
Fine.	好。	Hǎo.
And you?	你呢？	Nǐ ne?
Please ...	请……	Qǐng ...
Thank you.	谢谢你。	Xièxie nǐ.
Excuse me.	劳驾。	Láojià.
Sorry.	对不起。	Duìbùqǐ.
Yes.	是。	Shì.
No.	不是。	Bùshì.

Do you speak English?
你会说
英文吗？　　　Nǐ huìshuō
　　　　　　　Yīngwén ma?

I don't understand.
我不明白。　　　Wǒ bù míngbái.

Eating & Drinking

I'd like ...
我要……　　　Wǒ yào ...

a table for two	一张两个人的桌子	yīzhāng liǎngge rén de zhuōzi
the drink list	酒水单	jiǔshuǐ dān
the menu	菜单	càidān
beer	啤酒	píjiǔ
coffee	咖啡	kāfēi

I don't eat ...
我不吃……　　　Wǒ bùchī ...

fish	鱼	yú
poultry	家禽	jiāqín
red meat	牛羊肉	niúyángròu

Cheers!
干杯！　　　Gānbēi!

That was delicious.
真好吃。　　　Zhēn hǎochī.

The bill, please!
买单！　　　Mǎidān!

Shopping

I'd like to buy ...
我想买……　　　Wǒ xiǎng mǎi ...

I'm just looking.
我先看看。　　　Wǒ xiān kànkan.

How much is it?
多少钱？　　　Duōshǎo qián?

That's too expensive.
太贵了。　　　　Tàiguì le.

Can you lower the price?
能便宜　　　　Néng piányi
一点吗？　　　yīdiǎn ma?

Emergencies

Help!
救命！　　　　Jiùmìng!

Go away!
走开！　　　　Zǒukāi!

Call a doctor!
请叫医生来！　　Qǐng jiào yīshēng lái!

Call the police!
请叫警察！　　　Qǐng jiào jǐngchá!

I'm lost.
我迷路了。　　　Wǒ mílù le.

I'm sick.
我生病了。　　　Wǒ shēngbìng le.

Where are the toilets?
厕所在哪儿？　　Cèsuǒ zài nǎr?

Time & Numbers

What time is it?
现在几点钟？　　Xiànzài jǐdiǎn zhōng?

It's (10) o'clock.
(十)点钟。　　　(Shí)diǎn zhōng.

Half past (10).
(十)点三十分。　(Shí)diǎn sānshífēn.

morning	早上	zǎoshang
afternoon	下午	xiàwǔ
evening	晚上	wǎnshàng
yesterday	昨天	zuótiān
today	今天	jīntiān
tomorrow	明天	míngtiān

1	一	yī
2	二/两	èr/liǎng
3	三	sān
4	四	sì
5	五	wǔ
6	六	liù
7	七	qī
8	八	bā
9	九	jiǔ
10	十	shí

Transport & Directions

Where's ...?
……在哪儿？　　... zài nǎr?

What's the address?
地址在哪儿？　　Dìzhǐ zài nǎr?

How do I get there?
怎么走？　　　　Zěnme zǒu?

How far is it?
有多远？　　　　Yǒu duō yuǎn?

Can you show me on the map?
请帮我找　　　Qǐng bāngwǒ zhǎo
它在地图上　　tā zài dìtú shàng
的位置。　　　de wèizhi.

When's the next bus?
下一趟车　　　Xià yītàng chē
几点走？　　　jǐdiǎn zǒu?

A ticket to ...
一张到　　　　Yīzhāng dào
……的票。　　... de piào.

Does it stop at ...?
在……能下　　Zài ... néng xià
车吗？　　　　chē ma?

I want to get off here.
我想这儿下车。　Wǒ xiǎng zhèr xiàchē.

Index

See also separate subindexes for:

Eating p154
Drinking p155
Entertainment p155
Shopping p155

Sights p000
Map Pages **p000**

Sights p000
Map Pages **p000**

Sights p000
Map Pages **p000**

Behind the Scenes

Send Us Your Feedback

We love to hear from travellers – your comments help make our books better. We read every word, and we guarantee that your feedback goes straight to the authors. Visit **lonelyplanet.com/contact** to submit your updates and suggestions.

Note: We may edit, reproduce and incorporate your comments in Lonely Planet products such as guidebooks, websites and digital products, so let us know if you don't want your comments reproduced or your name acknowledged. For a copy of our privacy policy visit lonelyplanet.com/privacy.

Damian's Thanks

Thanks to Dai Min, Margaux, Alvin and Edward, Chris Pitts, Daniel Mc-Crohan, David Eimer, Edward Li, John Zhang, Jimmy Gu and Liu Meina. Much gratitude also to Jiale and Jiafu for everything, as always. Last but not least, a big thanks, of course, to the people of Shànghǎi for making their city so fascinating.

Acknowledgments

Cover photograph: Taichi on the Bund, Shànghǎi, Jon Arnold/AWL

This Book

This 4th edition of Lonely Planet's *Pocket Shànghǎi* guidebook was researched and written by Damian Harper. The previous two editions were written by Christopher Pitts. This guidebook was produced by the following:

Destination Editor Megan Eaves **Product Editors** Grace Dobell, Amanda Williamson **Regional Senior Cartographer** Julie Sheridan **Book Designer** Cam Ashley **Assisting Editors** Sarah Bailey, Victoria Harrison, Sally O'Brien **Assisting Author** Dai Min

Cover Researcher Naomi Parker **Thanks to** Cheree Broughton, Glenn Carter, Ryan Evans, Claire Murphy, Wayne Murphy, Kirsten Rawlings, Alison Ridgway, Samantha Russell-Tulip, Dianne Schallmeiner, Victoria Smith, Angela Tinson, Lauren Wellicome

Our Writer

Damian Harper

After graduating with a degree in modern and classical Chinese from London's School of Oriental and African Studies, guidebook writer Damian has lived and worked in Shànghǎi, Běijīng and Hong Kong, travelling the highways and byroads of China. Fascinated by China's coming of age, relishing Shànghǎi's finest xiǎolóngbāo dumplings and shíkùmén buildings, and while hounded by deadlines, Damian has written and updated multiple editions of guidebooks on Shànghǎi for Lonely Planet.

Published by Lonely Planet Publications Pty Ltd
ABN 36 005 607 983
4th edition – Apr 2016
ISBN 978 1 74321 565 4
© Lonely Planet 2016   Photographs © as indicated 2016
10 9 8 7 6 5 4 3 2 1
Printed in China